The Mighty Montagus

Earls of Salisbury and Kings of Man, 1301-1428

Derek Winterbottom

Alondra Books

All rights reserved. No part of this publication may be reproduced, stored in a retrieval system or transmitted in any form or by any means - electronic, photocopying, recording or otherwise - unless the written permission of the publishers has been obtained beforehand.

Published 2017
Reprinted 2018

Published by
Alondra Books
37 King Edward Bay, Isle of Man IM3 2JG

Printed and bound by
The Copy Shop
Douglas, Isle of Man

ISBN No. 978-0-9567540-3-5

Contents

Preface	3
Background	
The medieval kingdoms of England, Scotland and France	7
The kings of Man	10
The Early Montagus	
Simon and William, first and second lords Montagu, 1259-1319	15
William Montagu, first Earl of Salisbury, 1301-1344	
Early life, 1301-1330	30
The Nottingham coup, 1330	37
The grant of the Isle of Man, 1333	41
Earl of Salisbury, 1337	47
The start of the 'Hundred Years War', 1337	50
Crowned king in the Isle of Man, 1342	57
Campaigns in Brittany, 1343	61
The Feast of the Round Table and Salisbury's death, January, 1344	63
Did Edward III rape Salisbury's wife?	69
William Montagu, second Earl of Salisbury, 1328-1397	
Crécy and Calais, 1346-1347	72
The Garter, plague and 'divorce', 1347-1349	77
The loss of several Montagu estates	81
Poitiers and Brétigny, 1356-1360	84
Years of peace, 1360-1369	90
War again, 1369-1382	96
A new reign, 1377	100
Family tragedy and quarrels, 1381-1390	105
The sale of the Isle of Man, 1392	111

John Montagu, third Earl of Salisbury, 1350-1400
    Early life   116
    Supporter of Richard II, 1397-1399   120
    Enemy of Henry IV, 1399   127

Thomas Montagu, fourth Earl of Salisbury, 1388-1428
    Rise from disgrace, 1399-1409   131
    The road to Agincourt, 1409-1415   134
    From Agincourt to Baugé, 1415-1422   140
    Famous commander, 1422-1428   145

Aftermath
    The Neville earldom of Salisbury   156
    The fate of Bisham priory   159

Appendix
    Later Earls of Salisbury   161
    The later Montagus   162

Genealogical Chart   *166*

Sources   *167*

Reference Notes   *170*

Index   *175*

Acknowledgements

Many thanks for help and guidance to staff at the Institute of Historical Research, University of London; Manx National Heritage, Douglas; the National Portrait Gallery, London, and the Copy Shop, Douglas.

Front Cover

A very fine miniature model painted to represent the fourth Earl of Salisbury, fully equipped for war. Part of the St Petersburg Collection by Aero Art International, 11797 Hollyview Drive, Great Falls, VA 22066-1333, USA.

Preface

I wanted to research this book because, as someone who has written about the Isle of Man and its history, I was keen to know much more about the two Montagus who were kings of Man between 1333 and 1392. The Island records for the period are very sparse and the Montagus themselves have attracted little attention from biographers. The most detailed surveys of the family have been two unpublished London University theses, the M.A. of Robert Douch, presented in 1950, and the Ph.D. of Mark Warner, presented in 1991. Robert Douch was mostly concerned to show why it was possible for the first Earl of Salisbury to climb from the lower baronage to the highest ranks of the nobility through the king's favour, while Mark Warner's special interest was the outstanding military career of Thomas, the fourth earl. Neither was concerned with the Isle of Man, which they barely mention, but I could not have produced this book without constant reference to their admirable researches.

I have written little that is not already known, admittedly in very rarefied academic circles, about the medieval earls of Salisbury. But I have, I hope, joined up a lot of the links that already existed in order to create a clearer and fuller picture of members of the family and their careers. What has surprised me most is the fact that the Montagus emerge as being amongst the most influential men of their respective generations. Simon, the first Lord Montagu, 'conquered' the Isle of Man, his son was a favoured ally of Edward II and governor of the king's possessions in Gascony, while his grandson, the first Earl of Salisbury, was Edward III's closest personal friend and most influential confidant for a quarter of a century. The second earl was at Crécy and the siege of Calais, distinguished himself at Poitiers and lived long enough to be at the side of the young Richard II when he confronted Wat Tyler in the Peasants' Revolt of 1388. On top of this, he was the sovereign of Man for nearly half a century and he was personally responsible for the reconstruction of Castle Rushen, the Island's most iconic heritage site today, as well as many of the fortifications at Peel. This is not widely appreciated on the Island, as I think it should be.

The third earl was a crusader, a troubadour and a Lollard and he died violently in a futile attempt to restore to the throne the man he regarded as the rightful king. His son the fourth earl was an outstanding soldier hailed even in his own lifetime as the finest English commander in the French wars, saving only Henry V. Had he not died as the result of a freak cannon shot while besieging Orléans, he might well have captured the city and history might never have heard of Joan of Arc. So here we have six generations of continuous high achievers, which is comparatively rare for any family, I suspect.

There is a lot we cannot know about the period and we have to rely a good deal on guesswork. Ian Mortimer dropped a bombshell in 2003 by asserting in his biography of Roger Mortimer, Earl of March, (no relation, apparently) that Edward II was not murdered in Berkeley Castle after all and that he was spirited away, with the knowledge of his wife and son, to live the life of a hermit abroad. Mortimer's arguments are very persuasive, but we cannot be certain. Nor do we really know what lies behind the 'rape of the countess of Salisbury' story, or why a garter was chosen as the emblem for Edward III's chivalric order. Equally, it is not entirely clear when the first earl took possession of the lordship of Man and whether or not it was under English control in 1333 when the king granted it to him.

Students of medieval history have to accept that it is very difficult to know what the great men and women of the day looked like. Portraying a true likeness in artistic forms was not fashionable until the late fourteenth century and even literary descriptions are few and far between and tend to portray the subject as either a villain or a saint. It is likely that the first Earl of Salisbury was one-eyed after an accident or wound but beyond that it is difficult to say how members of the family would have appeared, except perhaps that they were generally young. The fourteenth century in Britain and France was a young person's world: you could be married in your early teens, succeed to a great inheritance by twenty-one, have reared a large family by thirty and have died on average before forty. The second Earl of Salisbury, who died aged 68, was a very old man for his time. It was also a brutal age, where beheadings and disembowellings were the regular order of the day, where the citizens of defeated towns were massacred and women raped as a matter of right. Yet atrocities such as this, and far worse, are still a part of our contemporary world, so we cannot be too censorious. It was also an age of revolution in men's fashions: the long, flowing robes of earlier centuries disappeared and men donned short jackets and tight-fitting hose that, like the lycra sports shorts of today, left little to the imagination. No wonder that churchmen denounced their wearers (ineffectively) as 'harlots'.

The fourteenth century saw 'Chivalry' reach its high point and there are certainly selective examples of courtesy, gentleness and fair-mindedness to be observed among the regular acts of barbarity. It was also an age of flamboyance and colour among the nobility as exampled by the court of Edward III, with its beautiful women and young knights and exciting tournaments and extravagant costumes all set against the magnificent backdrop of Windsor and other fine castles. But this was for the few: the many toiled in the fields or worked in unhealthy towns and considered that the chance of life as an archer in the lord's army was a welcome release. For the nobility, fighting was the only acceptable option. Servants ran their estates, clerks looked after their finances and for social reasons they could not involve themselves too much with commerce, while only younger sons would enter the church. If, as a noble, you served your king loyally and were lucky in battle, you could benefit in wealth and fortune and status: but you could also fall equally fast if your luck ran out. The Montagus experienced both sides of this particular coin.

The most impressive aspects of the fourteenth century in Britain and France were surely the Christian 'gothic' cathedrals which had developed since Norman times in the main towns, and the vast majority of them can be admired still, though the plain, Protestant interiors of today are very different from the highly-coloured walls, gilded carvings and painted columns of medieval times. Many castles, great and small, have survived so that no great leap of imagination is needed to recreate the world to which they were central, while many a museum and historic house harbours a suit of knightly armour.

There are many ongoing arguments about the period which will probably never be resolved. One is the name given to the 'Hundred Years War' which allegedly opened in 1337 and closed in 1453, which is 116 years, in any case. It seems to me that it was really two main wars, one running from 1337 to the treaty of Bruges in 1375, during which Edward III heroically gained and then lost a French empire, and the other running from 1415 to 1453 during which Henry V and the Duke of Bedford and his successors did the same. Another argument is whether the war was worth all the expense, loss of life and wanton destruction of French territory that it involved. The Victorians on the whole thought not, but in recent years British historians have tended to see Edward III as a very great ruler once more – 'The Perfect King', for Ian Mortimer, though Jonathan Sumption sees him as 'A Heroic Failure'. Mark Ormrod, who must know more about Edward III than anyone currently alive, takes a more balanced, though generally favourable, view in his marvellous biography, a colossal achievement in more ways than one. I am very grateful to these writers and all those in my list of sources, not only for providing me with the material with which to write this book, but for many hours of very enjoyable reading.

Derek Winterbottom
The Isle of Man
September 2017

Background

The medieval kingdoms of England, France and Scotland

The Romans maintained peace and an advanced civilisation in 'Britannia' for the best part of four hundred years but when they left in 410 much of the former province was soon colonized by Germanic peoples (Angles, Saxons and Jutes) who set up several small kingdoms such as Kent, Wessex, Mercia and Northumbria. These spent most of their time fighting each other until Viking raiders arrived in the ninth century and eventually forced the Anglo-Saxons to unite for protection under Alfred of Wessex (871-899). His grandson Athelstan (924-939) brought the Viking territories in the east of Britain under his control and he was able to claim to rule all England. This Anglo-Saxon-Viking kingdom prospered in relative isolation from Europe until it was conquered in 1066 by an army of warriors equipped with cavalry and led by William, the ambitious ruler of the small duchy of Normandy in northern France.

This 'Norman Conquest' drastically changed the nature of England because William claimed all the land (except that of the Church) as his own and granted it to his Norman supporters in return for a vow of homage which pledged them to provide military support whenever he called for it. Moreover, he encouraged his 'tenants' to build castles throughout the land (none had existed before) and he gave them, whether great lords or lesser knights, legal rights amounting to absolute control over the local population. This system, called 'feudalism' by much later historians, was adapted from developments on the continent. The conquest brought England into the main stream of western European life because the Norman ruling classes were linguistically and culturally French and from 1066 onwards the kings of England were also rulers of parts of France.

The Romans had ruled 'Gallia' for five centuries until a Germanic tribe known as the Franks eventually replaced them around 500, and 'Francia' became the most powerful kingdom in western Europe. In 768 Charles 'the Great', (or 'Charlemagne') became its ruler and he spent most of his life conquering his neighbours. He became king of Italy in 774 and then extended his rule into many of the Germanic lands so that in 800 he was crowned by the Pope as the first 'Holy Roman Emperor'. His empire failed to remain united after his death in 814 and split into several units. Count Odo of Paris was elected by his nobles as king of the western Franks in 888 and when he died ten years later Charles III (the Simple) was elected as his successor and it was he who in 911 granted an invading Viking warrior, Rollo, the right to settle in northern France. Even so, it was clearly understood that the 'dux Normannorum', the leader or 'duke' of Normandy was a 'vassal' of the king of France, owing him homage and fealty.

In 987 Hugh Capet, Duke of France and Count of Paris, was elected king of the Franks and his descendants the Capetians, the Valois and the Bourbons reigned in France for over 800 years. During most of the medieval period the king had direct personal control over only a limited area in the middle of the country, centred on Paris, though he claimed sovereign rights over the rulers of the many semi-independent lordships within France. Normandy and its surrounding provinces were often held by the kings of England, while Aquitaine, a large province in south-west France had once been a separate kingdom and was ruled by its own semi-autonomous dukes. When Henry II of England, the great-grandson of William I, married Eleanor, Duchess of Aquitaine in her own right, in 1154, this created the so-called 'Angevin empire'. Henry inherited the dukedom of Normandy and the counties of Anjou, Touraine and Maine from his father Geoffrey Plantagenet, Count of Anjou, and then the kingdom of England through his mother, followed by Aquitaine through marriage. He was also granted the title 'Lord of Ireland' by the Pope. His family was known as 'Plantagenet' because a yellow species of broom, 'planta genetica', common in Anjou, was the family emblem.

Philip II, who became King of the Franks in 1180 and ruled for 43 years, devoted his life with considerable success to the destruction of this Plantagenet grip on his country, helped by the unpopularity of Henry II's youngest son, King John. At his death in 1216 John had lost control of most of the Angevin territory in France except for Aquitaine, (also known as Guyenne or Gascony) so that Philip was the first of the Capetian kings who felt able to style himself 'King of France'. John's son, Henry III, made unsuccessful attempts to recover the lost territories and his son, Edward I, strengthened English control over Gascony by constructing new towns, or 'bastides'. English rule in Gascony was a constant cause of friction between the kings of France and England because the Capetians demanded a personal vow of homage for it, which the Plantagenets were reluctant to give because of its implied subservience. Also the French kings, as overlords, claimed the right to settle disputes between the king of England and his vassals in Gascony.

The Romans never conquered the Gaelic peoples of northern Britain and in the second century they built two garrisoned walls to stop the constant invasion of northern 'barbarians'. By the fifth century the two most important Gaelic peoples were the Picts in the north-east and the Scots in the west, and they fought each other until united under the Pictish leader, Kenneth MacAlpin, in 843, after which a kingdom of 'Alba', later called Scotland, came into precarious existence. After the Norman Conquest William I threatened Scotland but was content in 1072 to make a treaty of peace with Malcolm III (successor of Macbeth) who recognized William as his overlord and performed homage to him. Hence from this time onwards the kings of England claimed overlordship over Scotland, a fact the Scots ignored whenever they could.

The border between the two countries remained ill-defined and raids and invasions from both sides, either formal or informal, were frequent. David I, one of Scotland's most successful rulers, encouraged Norman knights to settle in Scotland, among them the famous families of de Brus, Fitzalan, Balliol, Comyn, Graham and Lindsay. David constructed royal castles on the English model, improved central administration and encouraged the building of monasteries. King William 'the Lion' (1165-1214) was defeated and captured by Henry II of England in 1174 and released only after once more performing homage to him for the Scottish kingdom. Yet the Scottish border remained constantly in dispute with the English, even after a treaty with them in 1237 in theory put it close to where it is today.

By 1300 the three kingdoms of France, England and Scotland were firmly established, but they were very different. The total population of France in 1300 has been estimated roughly at about 17 million, while England's was about four million and Scotland's less than one million. Paris was one of the largest cities in Europe, with about 200,000 citizens, followed by the much smaller Rouen. Orléans, Tours,

Bordeaux, Lyon, Dijon, Reims, Metz and Strasbourg all had more than 10,000 citizens. By contrast, London had about 80,000 citizens in 1300, followed by York with about 22,000 and Bristol with between 15-20,000, but most of England's other towns had very small populations. In 1300 Edinburgh was still a small town which did not even receive a royal charter until 1329.

By 1300 most towns were surrounded with stout walls reinforced by towers, many of them painted white. Carcassonne is perhaps the best preserved walled town in France (though heavily restored) while in Britain the most impressive walled town is probably Conwy in Wales, followed by York. Within the town walls there would be many churches and a few impressive public buildings but most domestic dwellings were very basic and conditions were extremely insanitary. The countryside was dotted with castles of varying sizes, some of them complex and magnificent, others simply practical. By far the most impressive, indeed breathtaking, features of both England and France were the magnificent 'gothic' cathedrals whose flying buttresses and pinnacles soared skywards in a way which is stunning today, let alone then. It is no wonder that the Roman Christian church held a very tight grip on a largely illiterate and superstitious population.

The kings of Man

For more than 350 years (from c. 900 to 1265) the Isle of Man was the central part of a scattered island kingdom ruled by its own kings of Viking origin. During this period these kings managed to maintain a very considerable degree of independence while at the same time acknowledging the superior status of the more powerful rulers of the larger states bordering on the Irish Sea. King Edgar of England (959-975) was crowned and anointed in 973 in Bath - the first formal coronation of a king of all England in a ceremony that has remained relatively unchanged. According to the chronicler Florence of Worcester:

> Shortly afterwards he sailed round the north coast of Britain with a large fleet and landed at Chester. He was met, as he had given orders, by eight tributary kings, namely Kenneth, king of the Scots, Malcolm, king of the Cumbrians, Maecus, king of several isles, and five

others...who swore fealty and bound themselves to military service by land and sea. Attended by them, King Edgar one day went on board a boat, and while they plied the oars, he took the helm and steered skilfully down the course of the river Dee, and followed by his whole retinue of earls and nobles pursued the voyage from the palace to the monastery of St John the Baptist. Having paid his devotions there, he returned to the palace with the same pomp. He is reported as having said to his nobles as he entered the gates that any successor of his might truly boast of being King of England when he should receive such honours, with so many kings doing him homage.[1]

Other chronicles number the oarsmen kings as only six, with the other three hailing mostly from Gwynedd (North Wales), but it is almost certain that 'Maecus', or Magnus, was a king of Man and the Isles.

Edgar did not long enjoy his pre-eminent status because he died in 975, aged only 32, but this episode makes it quite clear that a kingly ruler of islands in the Irish Sea was already well known and respected, though we know very little about who these early Scandinavian Manx kings were and what they achieved. The first well-documented king of Man is Godred Crovan, (1079-1095), a Viking with Irish connections, because the 'Chronicle of the Kings of Man and the Isles', the main Manx source for the early medieval period, begins its account of Manx affairs in 1016 and describes Godred's conquest of the Island around 1079 in considerable detail and explains how he subsequently extended his influence in the western isles and in the region round Dublin. The chronicle, written by monks of Rushen Abbey around 1262, then gives an often bloodthirsty account of the far from peaceful lives and reigns of Godred's successors, most of whom were his direct descendants. At its high point the extensive sea kingdom consisted of Man and most of the islands off the north-west coast of Scotland except for the Orkneys, until a civil war led to the loss of the Islay and Mull group of islands to Scottish lords from 1164 onwards.

By the reign of Reginald I (1187-1228) the kings of Man had built up a considerable fleet, an important asset which made them a force to be reckoned with in the Irish Sea. Reginald attacked County Down in Ireland with 100 ships in 1204, which led King John of England to make him an ally in return for financial and territorial rewards but in 1210 when Reginald sided with John's enemies in Ireland, John despatched an English force which ravaged Man. This led to Reginald doing formal homage to John in 1212. During the minority of John's successor, Henry III, Reginald again attacked Ireland and switched his allegiance from the king of England to Pope Honorius III, becoming a papal vassal. Reginald was killed in 1228 by his younger brother, who ruled as Olaf II (1228-1237). Faced with other challengers for the Manx throne he sought support by doing homage first of all to Haakon IV, the ruler of Norway in its 'golden age', and then to Henry III of England. Henry was prepared to pay Olaf 40 marks and large quantities of corn and wine in return for his promise to guard English shipping and provide a fleet of 50 ships for Henry, if necessary. When Olaf died in 1237 his son Harald I was faced with an invasion by Haakon, who exercised what he considered were his claims to Man by sending an army to take possession of it until Harald would recognize Haakon as his overlord. Harald agreed and married Haakon's daughter Cecilia but they were both tragically drowned at sea while returning to Man in 1248.

Haakon then intervened decisively in a succession dispute over the Manx kingship and effectively governed the Island until Olaf II's youngest son, Magnus, was accepted by the Manx as king in 1252 as Haakon's vassal. He was able to rule peaceably until a new threat arose with the accession to the Scottish throne of an able young king, Alexander III, who was determined to capture all the western islands. He attacked Skye and this prompted an invasion of Scotland by Haakon, aided by his ally and vassal, Magnus of Man. An indecisive conflict at Largs was soon followed by the death of Haakon, so that Magnus had little choice but to do homage to Alexander for his island kingdom, which he would hold in return for hostages and ten war galleys whenever they were needed. Scottish chroniclers who described this occasion referred to Magnus as a kinglet (regulus) ruling a petty kingdom (regniculum).[2] When Magnus died in 1265 he left only an illegitimate son, Godred, which gave Alexander the opportunity to claim the Isle of Man for himself. In 1266 he signed the Treaty of Perth with the new king of Norway, who agreed to cede to him all rights over the kingdom of Man and the Isles for 1,000 marks a year for four years, and then 100 marks a year in perpetuity. It was further declared that in future the inhabitants of Man and the Isles would be subject to the laws and customs of Scotland.

The Treaty of Perth therefore marked the end of the independent kingdom of Man, which was now formally annexed to Scotland.[3] The Manx themselves were far from happy about the change and indeed a rebellion led by Godred, an illegitimate son of Magnus, was defeated on the Island by a powerful Scottish force from Galloway in 1275. Fate, however, dealt the Scottish monarchy an unlucky hand. Alexander's son and heir died in 1284 and when he himself died in 1286 his only remaining heir was his grand-daughter Margaret, who died, aged seven, in 1290. Claims to the vacant Scottish throne were then put forward by some twelve individuals, while others claimed sovereignty over Man. One of these was Mary, the widow of Magnus, lately King of Man, and another was Affreca of Connacht, allegedly a cousin of Magnus.

In the vacuum created by the vacancy on the Scottish throne, Richard de Burgh, Earl of Ulster, took possession of the Isle of Man, probably on the orders of Edward I, King of England since 1272. A formal assembly of islanders asked for the protection of the king and he granted this and appointed Walter de Huntercombe as the Island's custodian. Edward's chief interest in the Island at this particular time was very likely to have been as a source of lead for the castles he was then constructing in North Wales as part of his determination to incorporate the rebellious Welsh into his English kingdom. To resolve the dispute over the Scottish kingship the various interested parties in Scotland reluctantly agreed to recognize Edward as their 'superior lord' and asked him to adjudicate between the many rival claimants. After lengthy deliberations he chose John Balliol in 1292 and dutifully handed the Isle of Man back to him the following year, recognizing that it was a Scottish possession. In 1295 Balliol contracted a momentous alliance of mutual security with Philip IV, King of France, by which both countries pledged to support the other, if attacked. This came to be known as the 'Auld Alliance' and remained the corner-stone of Franco-Scottish policy for the next 250 years.

Peace between England and Scotland was shattered in 1296 when Scottish nobles forced King John Balliol to rebel against Edward, largely because they resented the English king's authority and what they

The Isle of Man, strategically important in the Irish sea.

considered his excessive demands as their 'superior lord'. Edward's famous response, earning him his reputation as 'the hammer of the Scots', was to march an army into Scotland where he defeated the Scots that year at Dunbar. King John abdicated, had his royal surcoat ripped from him by Anthony Bek, the bishop of Durham, and was taken to London in captivity. Also the enthronement Stone of Scone was removed to Westminster and the Scottish crown presented to the shrine of St Thomas Becket in Canterbury. John Balliol eventually went into exile in France, where he died in 1314. He made no further attempt to regain the Scottish throne and Edward I determined to rule Scotland through governors, though Scottish resistance was heroically led after 1296 by William Wallace, until his capture and grisly execution in 1305. At this stage, it seemed that Edward I, who had firmly subjected Wales, had also succeeded in conquering Scotland. Even the Isle of Man was seized from the Scots in 1301 by an English lord, Simon Montagu.

The Early Montagus

Simon and William, first and second lords Montagu 1259-1319

Drogo or Dreu, a knight who hailed from Montaigue in Normandy, came to England at the time of the Norman Conquest in 1066 in the retinue of Duke William's half-brother Robert, Count of Mortain, whose friend and trusted companion Drogo is said to have been. In the Domesday Book (1086) 'Drogo de Montagud' is recorded as holding the manors of Donyatt and Shipton Montagu (Somerset) from the count. Various theories exist concerning the origin of the family name and how it should be spelt, and the two main variants are Montagu and Montacute. In his London MA thesis (1950) Robert Douch, who later became an authority on the local history of the West Country, argues convincingly that the name Shipton 'Montagu', the original manor which remained in the family's possession for some four hundred years, almost certainly derives from the name of its lord, Drogo de Montagud, and that the name 'Montacute' derives from scribes who wrote the French name 'Montaigue' in Latin as 'Monte Acuto'.[4] The name probably does not derive from the hamlet of Montacute in Somerset where Robert of Mortain built a motte-and-bailey castle on top of a pointed hill (also written in Latin as 'monte acuto'). Later a priory was founded close by but not until 1598 was the well-known Montacute House built there by the Phelips family, long after the 'mighty Montagus' were dead and gone.

The Montagus did not rise rapidly to prominence and records of their early history are sparse. Drogo's grandson, Richard de Montagu, granted lands to Bruton Priory in Somerset during the decade of the 1160s. A William de Montagu was sheriff of Somerset and Dorset from 1204 to 1207 and became a powerful figure as one of King John's justiciars in 1208, the first time a Montagu rose to national importance. His grandson, also William, fought in Wales with Henry III's eldest son, later Edward I, in 1255 and was summoned for service regularly until 1264.[5]

Simon Montagu was this William's son by his wife Berthe and he was born around 1259. He was a child when his father died in 1270, the year he was formally married to Hawise, the daughter of Amaury de St Armand, but seven years later he was fighting for Edward I in Wales, and again in 1282. By this stage he was regarded by the king as a significant force, because he was summoned to the parliament held the following year at Shrewsbury. As he would have been in the category of baron rather than a knight, this has led to him being referred to as the first 'Lord Montagu'. At this time he held considerable lands outside Somerset because in 1290, as part of Edward's great 'Quo Warranto' inquiry into land holdings, he surrendered all his properties in Dorset, Devon, Buckinghamshire and Oxfordshire to the king, receiving them back by royal charter (and payment of a no doubt hefty sum to the exchequer). He fought in Gascony between 1294 and 1297 and took a ship full of supplies through a line of French galleys to relieve the besieged town of Bourg-sur-Mer in 1296. In 1298 he attended the parliament at York where Edward I planned his Scottish campaign and he became jointly custodian of Corfe Castle in 1299. In the Scottish campaign of that year he served as a household banneret – a knight who commanded other knights – and he was present at the siege of Caerlaverock in 1300, when a small force of Scottish defenders valiantly held out against the might of Edward I's army. By his wife Hawise, or possibly his second wife Isabella, of whom little is known, Simon had two sons, named, in the family tradition, William and Simon.[6]

In 1301, Simon paid for the equipping of a galley, a barge and a hundred men in order to serve Edward I in the naval war against Scotland around the Western Isles. It seems that part of Simon's campaign, in which he was assisted by his elder son William, then sixteen, included the successful conquest of the Isle of Man from its Scottish defenders. However, the expense of this venture proved too much for the Montagu finances and Simon agreed to mortgage the Island for seven years to Anthony Bek, the bishop of Durham, a trusted friend and supporter of Edward I. Bek formally styled himself 'Lord of Man' from 1301 but, as a celibate priest, he could be lord only for his lifetime and Simon Montagu still nourished hope that his claim to the Island would eventually be recognized. In 1302 he returned to Gascony to perform a year's military service.[7]

Meanwhile, Simon's elder son, William, born in 1285, was beginning to make his mark. Queen Eleanor had already arranged an early

The Early Montagus

marriage for him with Elizabeth Montford, a daughter of Sir Peter de Montford of Beaudesert in Warwickshire, and he became a valet in the king's household in 1299. In 1302, the year after he had helped his father capture the Isle of Man, we find him, at the age of seventeen, described as a 'king's yeoman' and placed, together with a certain Peter of Dunwich, in charge of ships being prepared for Edward I's Scottish war, tasked with ensuring that they were properly equipped with men and arms. The following year the Earl of Pembroke paid William Montagu a considerable compliment by describing him as one 'who has done good service to the king and whom he cannot spare without grievous loss from his company' and he requested the Chancellor to intervene with local justices to save Montagu from a writ of novel disseisin concerning some of his land in Hertfordshire.[8] He was with the king at the siege of Stirling in 1304 and helped to provision the army with pikes, 'stonhaxes' and engines of war.

In 1305 the elusive 'Affreca of Connacht' formally transferred by quitclaim all her rights in the Isle of Man to Simon Montagu and notified all her tenants on the Island that they owed fealty to him. Some historians have argued that this was because she became his third wife, though this is disputed. It is not even clear who she actually was, though some chroniclers considered her to be related to Magnus, the last Scandinavian king of Man, whose heiress she claimed to be. Though this aspect of Affreca is vague, the transfer of her rights on the Island to Simon Montagu is well documented and it meant that he could claim, in theory, that the Island was rightfully his by both conquest and inheritance. That the Isle of Man was a very valuable prize, (apart from the titular kingship) and well worth fighting for is emphasized by records which show that Bishop Bek owed the king a thousand marks in rent for the Island and that he appointed a justiciar and bailiffs to administer it and collect the substantial revenues due to him.[9]

In the same year Simon's son, William, seems to have got himself into some degree of trouble because he was imprisoned in the Tower of London with his uncle Amaury de St Armand and others, 'accused of having detained Alicia de Droys, although she was pregnant, and they had declared John of Kent dead and set him free. They also repelled the sheriff of Oxford from Oxford castle. William's father stood surety and he was quickly released...' A jury later found William and Amaury guilty of no crime.[10]

In 1306 Robert Bruce, Earl of Carrick, whose grandfather had been one of the unsuccessful claimants to the Scottish throne in 1290, revived the Scottish rebellion against Edward I by proclaiming himself king of the Scots but he was forced to flee to the Western Isles after the initial failure of this 'coup'. Later that year William Montagu was one of three hundred young men who were knighted after Edward I's son and heir, Edward of Caernarfon, received his spurs on the Feast of Pentecost, 22 May. It was proclaimed that anyone whose father was a knight and sought knighthood for himself should present himself in London before this date and receive the necessary equipment from the royal wardrobe. Edward II's biographer, Seymour Phillips, drawing his information mainly from the chronicler of the 'Flores Historiarum' has provided a lively account of what happened next:

> The future knights spent the night before in church, many of them in the Temple church but the more distinguished, including the Prince of Wales, in Westminster Abbey. Supposedly they were composing themselves in prayer for the chivalric duties they were about to assume: in fact there was so much noise and general excitement that the monks of Westminster were scarcely able to say their office in the choir of the abbey. On the following day, 22 May, Edward I knighted his son in the chapel of the palace of Westminster; the young Edward's spurs were attached to his heels by the two senior earls of the kingdom… Afterwards Edward went to Westminster Abbey where he knighted all the other young men, amounting altogether to about three hundred. The ceremony was marred by the great crowds of people within the abbey. Two knights were crushed to death, while other knights inside the abbey had to clear the way on horseback. The Prince of Wales, meanwhile, had to retreat to the high altar for safety.
>
> The ceremonies were followed by a great feast in Westminster Hall, during which the guests were entertained by over eighty minstrels drawn from the households of the king, queen and prince, and from the

service of many other nobles and clergy. The highlight of the feast, and the detail which most interested the chroniclers, was the oaths taken upon two swans by Edward I and the prince, followed by the other nobles and knights, that they would defeat Robert Bruce.... The mass knighting and the subsequent feast were exciting social events, some of the most exciting that England had ever known...[11]

The fourteenth century would be the high point of the 'Age of Chivalry' in Western Europe, when the greatest attention was paid by the upper classes to the perceived responsibilities and duties of the knight, a young man who should ideally be well-bred, handsome, courteous, brave, loyal, trustworthy, generous and devoted to a female patron. Naturally he was expected to be a valiant warrior, but also one who appreciated the finer things in life, such as music, poetry and dancing. The concept of chivalry had its roots far back in the legend of the (essentially fictitious) early British King Arthur and his knightly companions, a tale embellished and expanded by generations of poets and troubadours so that it had come to be generally accepted as historical fact. For young William Montagu, being knighted by his sovereign marked his formal entry into the charmed circle of the English aristocracy – a very small group. In an English population of about four million, there were generally about a dozen earls, about fifty barons and, by 1300, only about 1,200 knights. The number of knights dropped drastically from about 4,500 in 1200 because of the rise in the status of a knight and the consequent expense of maintaining his horses, armour, livery and entourage.[12] 'Chivalry' and its rules generally (but not always, by any means) applied to these upper classes, though not to the masses beneath them in the social scale.

In the early part of 1307 Simon Montagu, assisted by his son William, was appointed by Edward I to take charge of a fleet of fifteen ships based at Ayr which would patrol the North Channel and prevent Bruce from returning to Scotland. Also, William Montagu crossed to Ireland on a special mission to seek out supporters of Bruce, and he and three others were subsequently paid £10 for capturing several rebels and confining them in Dublin Castle.[13] Bruce did eventually get back to the mainland, but at a high cost when his two brothers were defeated in Galloway and beheaded.

To meet this new threat posed by Bruce, Edward I personally led another invading army to Scotland but contracted dysentery and died at Burgh-by-Sands in the summer of 1307. His death brought to an end a great reign which had seen the conquest of Wales and nearly the conquest of Scotland. In addition, the king's extensive possessions in south-western France had been consolidated and strengthened, while at home Edward's legal reforms had clarified and regularised ancient practice. It was widely accepted that this imposing man (standing six feet two inches tall), who had won acclaim as a crusader in his youth, had also been a master of the art of kingship. But, in addition to his great reputation, he left to his successor very considerable debts, high levels of taxation and a legacy of unfinished business in Scotland, where Robert Bruce was gaining support with every passing day.

The new king, Edward II, was the ninth child and fourth and only surviving son of his father by his much-loved wife, Eleanor, daughter of the Spanish king of Castile. Born in 1284, he was one year younger than William Montagu and twenty-three when he succeeded to the throne, by all accounts a handsome young man with a fine physique. His mother had died in 1290 and his father agreed a treaty with Philip IV of France in 1298 that he himself would marry Philip's sister, Margaret, and that his heir would marry Philip's daughter Isabella, then aged two. One year after succeeding to the throne, Edward II honoured this agreement and married Isabella in a splendid ceremony in Boulogne Cathedral in January 1308, following this with a magnificent joint coronation in Westminster Abbey. The new queen was still only twelve and the couple's first child, the future Edward III, was born in November 1312, when Isabella was sixteen, and three more children followed at regular intervals. The king also had an illegitimate son, Adam, born in 1307.

Despite this steady heterosexual performance, Edward had for many years been involved in an ambiguous relationship with a young French knight, Piers Gaveston. About the same age as Edward, Piers was the younger son of a Gascon lord who fought in the service of Edward I. Piers caught the old king's eye as a young man with impressive fighting skills and around 1300 the king chose him as a member of his son's household, seemingly as a role model. During the next few years the prince and Gaveston became very close companions and may have entered into a pact of chivalric brotherhood. By 1304 the king had enough confidence in Gaveston to agree to his son's request to grant him the wardship of Roger Mortimer of Wigmore, meaning that he had control of the young lord's upbringing and estates until he reached maturity.[14] But early in 1307 it was clear to the king that his son's friendship with Gaveston had gone far beyond reasonable bounds when the prince asked his father to invest Piers with his own county of Ponthieu, a great lordship in France, or possibly even the earldom of Cornwall. According to the chroniclers, the king was so enraged that he tore out fistfuls of his son's hair and banished Gaveston from the kingdom. This is not necessarily because he suspected the two of being lovers, but because in the aristocratic world of the time upstarts and favourites were almost always strongly resented.

When he lay dying, Edward I instructed his most trusted supporters to make sure that Gaveston stayed in exile but as soon as he was dead Edward II recalled him and created him Earl of Cornwall, which made him lord of most of that county, with many estates elsewhere in addition and a huge annual income of about £4,000. The king also arranged a prestigious marriage for Gaveston with Margaret de Clare, sister of the Earl of Gloucester, and left him as regent of the kingdom when he crossed to France to marry Isabella – a responsibility normally entrusted only to persons of royal rank. These foolish decisions alienated many of the great barons and at the coronation feast in London it was noticed that Edward paid far more attention to Gaveston than to his new wife while Gaveston's subsequent arrogance and rudeness to other great lords, for whom he invented unflattering nicknames, caused outrage. In June 1308 Edward was forced by baronial pressure to send Gaveston out of the kingdom, though he appointed him lieutenant of Ireland and soon called him back in 1309. Inevitably, this provoked renewed opposition from the hostile barons

In 1310 Edward attempted to deflect attention from his critics by resuming the war against Scotland and Gaveston went with him, as did William Montagu. The king promoted Simon Montagu to the rank of admiral and placed him in charge of a sizeable English fleet based in the Irish Sea to guard against a Scottish invasion. In December that year he wrote to Gilbert MacAskil, Bishop Bek's steward on the Isle of Man, authorizing him to collect men from north-western England to defend the Island. The king wrote:

> We understand from several sources that Robert Bruce, our enemy and traitor, is exerting pressure with his forces and intends to send his whole galley fleet from the Western Isles against the Isle of Man this winter to destroy that island and to seize for himself and his abettors, our enemies and rebels, all victuals and necessaries in the said Isle of Man and to use them for his own ends and to sustain his accomplices.[15]

No invasion materialised for the moment because Robert Bruce was not yet ready to take on the English and he carefully avoided a pitched battle in Scotland. Edward II ran out of money and supplies and returned to London in 1311, leaving Gaveston as lieutenant of Scotland.

Bishop Bek died in March that year, described by the Annals of London as bishop of Durham and 'rex Mannorum', or king of the Manx, and Simon Montagu seems to have regarded his death as an opportunity to strengthen the Montagu claim to the kingship of Man, possibly by taking control of Castle Rushen without the express permission of the king. This led to serious trouble when Dungal MacDowall, the custodian of the castle, brought charges against him before Edward II at Berwick, 'concerning felonies in the Isle of Man', which were described as an 'attempt to occupy the land of Man to the king's disinheritance'. His case was heard before the royal council: they found against him and he was committed to prison in Windsor later in the year.[16]

Several chronicles record that after the death of Bishop Bek Edward II intended to grant the Isle of Man to Piers Gaveston, possibly because it was a relatively safe place for Gaveston to reside at a time when he was under renewed attack from powerful baronial critics. These barons produced a series of 'Ordinances' in 1311, demanding reforms in the royal administration and in particular the exile of Gaveston. No record has survived of any grant of the Island to Gaveston, which might well have been blocked by the 'Lords Ordainers', as Edward's baronial opponents were known.[17] Edward was forced to send Gaveston into exile once more in November 1311 but in flagrant disregard of all his promises he recalled him only two months later. Losing patience, the hostile barons, led by the king's first cousin, Thomas, Earl of Lancaster, rebelled and took arms against the king and Gaveston, who was captured in May 1312. In Warwick Castle he was condemned without much of a trial by many earls and barons and taken out onto the Kenilworth Road, two miles out of Warwick, where the Earl of Lancaster 'handed him over to two Welshmen for execution. One of them ran him through the body and the other cut off his head'.[18] He was twenty-eight years old.

Edward II was distraught at the death of Gaveston and vowed revenge on those responsible for what he considered a murder in flagrant disregard of the laws and customs of the land of which he, the king, was the guardian. He blamed especially Thomas of Lancaster and a contest between these two and their supporters dominated English politics for the next ten years. Meanwhile, William Montagu rose steadily in the royal favour. In 1311 he was given the responsibility of surveying the castles at Hastings, Porchester, Old Sarum and Colchester and choosing custodians for them, while he himself became custodian of Berkhamsted Castle. In 1313 he was appointed to command the fleet which took the king and queen to France for an elaborate and extravagant state visit to the court of Philip IV.[19] Philip had recently struck down the powerful Order of Knights Templar in France and Edward II followed his example in England: Montagu was one of those chosen to witness the conveyance of the lands of the disgraced order to the Knights Hospitaller.[20] Also by 1313, possibly as a result of the rise in favour of his son, Simon Montagu had been released from prison in Windsor Castle and pardoned for his offences on the Isle of Man.[21]

The Montagus were still disappointed in their ambition to secure the lordship of the Isle of Man because in May 1311 it was next granted for life to Henry Beaumont, a loyal supporter of Edward II. This grant was overturned by the Ordainers but by 1312 Edward had recovered enough authority to issue another charter, granting the Island to Beaumont:

> with all its dominion and royal right, together with knight's fees, advowsons of churches and religious houses, liberties, free customs, escheats and all other appurtenances to hold by the service which the lords of

Man were accustomed to render to the kings of Scotland.²²

Gilbert Macaskil remained in charge of the administration while in February 1313 Dungal Macdowall, a Scottish opponent of the Bruce regime, returned to the Island and again took charge of the garrison at Castle Rushen. In 1307 Macdowall had been responsible for capturing two of Bruce's brothers and handing them over for execution and this may have been an additional reason why Bruce decided to attack the Island in May 1313 in order to recover it for the Scottish crown. According to the 'Chronicle of the Kings of Man and the Isles':

> In 1313 Robert, King of Scotland, landed with a large navy at Ramsey on 18 May and on the following Sunday he went to the monastery at Douglas, where he spent the night. On the Monday following he laid siege to Castle Rushen, which was held by Lord Duncan MacDowyl against the king, until the Tuesday after the festival of St Barnabas the apostle [12 June], when Lord Robert took the castle.²³

After this stout resistance, lasting a month, Macdowall managed to escape, but according to the Dublin chronicle the castle (which at that stage consisted only of a sturdy Anglo-Norman-style tower) was 'demolished', though this is likely to be an exaggeration.²⁴

In 1314 Edward II attempted to strike a decisive blow against Robert Bruce who, in addition to his conquest of the strategically important Isle of Man, had captured many Scottish castles loyal to Edward in the preceding years and whose position was by now extremely threatening. Early in the year the important fortress at Stirling was besieged by the Scots and its custodian agreed that it would surrender if not relieved by the summer. Edward rose to this challenge and assembled an impressive army of about two thousand cavalry and fifteen thousand infantry, many of them longbowmen. Marching up to Berwick, Edward and his army crossed into Scotland and arrived at Stirling on 23 June. An inconclusive skirmish was fought that day but after crossing the Bannock Burn and expecting the much smaller Scots force to withdraw, Edward's army was surprised and outmanoeuvered by a Scottish attack on the 24th. The English broke ranks and the Scottish infantry were able to kill large numbers of mounted knights. Edward, against his will, was forced to leave the field by his own supporters and managed to reach safety. Though this was a humiliating defeat, it did not end the Scottish war or result in the recognition by England of Robert Bruce as king of Scots.

After the calamity at Bannockburn, William Montagu was appointed to the post of warden, or captain, of Berwick-on-Tweed, the king's most important northern stronghold, a responsibility he fulfilled from August to November 1314. During this time he held an inquisition into two boys, aged eleven and nine, who were accused of 'trafficking with the Scottish rebels'. They had been discovered outside the town gate and when questioned, they said that they had been playing there and one of them had lost his rudiment song book. For fear of their master, the boys had gone to look for the book and been taken prisoner by the Scots, so they claimed. They were acquitted.[25] The following year William embarked upon an exploit which could have found its way into any troubadour's song of chivalry when he led a party of knights and esquires to rescue Lady de Clifford, who was reputed to have been raped at Barnard Castle by Henry de Irreys.[26]

Also in 1315 William held the post of captain of the knights of the king's household and he was given a command in the expedition of 1316 which was sent to deal with the rebellion of the Welsh leader Llewellyn Bren, who had attacked Caerphilly Castle in Glamorgan. Under the overall command of the Earl of Hereford, William Montagu and Hugh Audley were both appointed to lead a force of men-at-arms against Llewellyn in February and they were joined by other marcher lords so that by the next month Llewellyn had surrendered and been sent off to the Tower of London. A letter exists written by Montagu to the king, describing how Llewellyn was defeated. He wrote (in modernized English):

> Sir Henry de Lancaster, Sir John Giffard and we of your household rode on 12 March from Cardiff towards the castle of Caerphilly. We found there Llewellyn Bren with all his host in battle upon the summit of the mountain and they had dyked and fortified all roads to the castle, and we went to the end of the mountain a

good three leagues from the road and took the mountain and passed along it among their force and Llewellyn and a great part of his host took to flight and those who stayed were soon dead and discomfited, and then we went to the castle and garnished it sufficiently with people and victuals and took the lady out of the castle with us and on our return to Cardiff we beat down all the dykes and forts that they had made, by which we understand that the war will soon be finished.

Montagu ended with a request to the king 'to send us hastily a commission that I might take them unconditionally to your peace, and to succour us with money for wages, for we have at your wages, 150 men-at-arms and 2,000 footmen.' A commission was duly issued for Montagu and others to hold trials of those taking part in the rebellion and impose fines accordingly.[27] Later that year Montagu spent some time in Bristol, attempting to resolve a dispute between the city burgesses and the constable of the castle, Sir Bartholomew Badlesmere. The citizens resisted stoutly and eventually it was necessary for Badlesmere, Montagu and others to besiege the city, which surrendered after about a week.[28]

William Montagu's rise in royal favour was marked in 1316 by the grant to him of the right to arrange the marriage of Joan, daughter and heiress of Theobald of Verdun, and late in the year he was appointed to the influential post of steward of the royal household, which marked his entry to Edward II's closest circle. By this time he had become the second Lord Montagu because his father, Simon, died in September at the age of 56 and was buried in Bruton Priory, Somerset, which had been patronised by the Montagus for some 150 years. The following year, the marriage took place between William's eldest son John and Joan of Verdun, but John died, still a boy, only four months later and his funeral was held in Lincoln Cathedral in August 1317. The king's regard for the Montagus at this time of family tragedy is shown by the fact that Edward provided two pieces of taffeta and one piece of Lucca cloth, all costly items, to be laid upon young John's body and also paid for forty clerics to pray for his soul, thirteen widows to watch over his body before burial, friars of Lincoln to say Masses for his soul and the distribution of alms to the local poor.[29]

Two miniature models painted to represent William, the second Lord Montagu (mounted) and a man-at-arms, both displaying the Montagu arms on their shields - (Argent, three fusils conjoined in fess gules) i.e. three red lozenges on a silver or white background. The figures are only about an inch high. Courtesy of Matthew Perks.

The influence of William Montagu over the king was so evident by this time that he received a letter from Pope John XXII in May 1317 urging him and others to do all in their power to pacify the realm, to help the king, to afford justice and to prevent any oppression of the church and her ministers.[30] The Pope's concern resulted from the fact that the kingdom had been very restless since the death of Gaveston, divided between the king's critics, led by Thomas of Lancaster, and his supporters. The disaster at Bannockburn had only strengthened the case of those who regarded Edward as an incompetent ruler, unable to choose wise councillors or to defeat his foreign enemies. To add to this, from 1314 onwards, England, together with much of northern Europe, suffered from exceptionally bad weather, consisting of heavy rains and cold winters, which ruined successive harvests and caused famine for almost the biblical span of seven years. The popular mindset of the time was disposed to see this calamity as a divine verdict on a worthless ruler, which significantly added to Edward's difficulties.

Increasingly the king turned for support to a small group of advisers who were not drawn from the greater baronage. By 1317 the most influential of these were probably Hugh d'Audley, Roger Damory and William Montagu, though Hugh Despencer and his son, also named Hugh, were waiting in the wings, full of ambition. The king's confidence in Montagu is reflected in the gifts he heaped upon him in 1317. He was granted an annuity of 200 marks in February in return for contracting to serve the king for life, an agreement also made by Roger Damory. He received manors in Gravesend, Kent, and Kingsbury, Somerset, in June, money from the fee farms of Chichester and Rochester and a tenement and a quay on the banks of the Thames in London. He was also granted the lands of a rebel, William de Carlisle, and his tenant Simon of Goseford, the ransoms of three Welsh rebels, lands in Norfolk, Somerset and Devon, and finally a licence to crenellate his main house at Cassington in Oxfordshire. Then, in 1318, he was appointed keeper of Abingdon Abbey and absolved from paying the debts of his late father.[31]

This marked the zenith of William's political influence because towards the end of 1318 he was transferred from his position as steward of the household to the theoretically more prestigious post of seneschal of Gascony and Aquitaine, making him the chief royal officer in south-west France. This appointment, which effectively removed Montagu from English politics, marked a victory for Thomas of Lancaster who regarded Montagu as a dangerous enemy he publicly accused of trying to kill him. Montagu had certainly accused Lancaster of treachery at a council held at Clarendon in February 1317 and the pro-Lancaster author of the 'Flores Historiarum' described Montagu as having risen 'in the king's shadow' and being a worse political influence even than Gaveston.[32] Montagu's loyal support, steady advice and military experience were a serious loss to the king, who now turned more and more for advice to the greedy and ambitious Despensers, with what proved to be disastrous results.

As for the Isle of Man, it seemed even less likely by now that it would ever fall into Montagu hands. Robert Bruce's conquest of the Manx and capture of Castle Rushen in 1313 was temporarily reversed in 1315 when the Island was recaptured by a Scottish rebel, Ewan of Argyll, but in 1316 Robert Bruce granted the Island to Thomas Randolph, Earl of Moray, who took possession of it by the end of 1317 and was able to hold on to it for the next fifteen years.[33]

William Montagu, first Earl of Salisbury, 1301-1344

Early life, 1301-1330

The second Lord Montagu died while seneschal of Gascony in 1319 under unknown circumstances, aged only 34. His widow, Elizabeth, was a generous benefactor of the priory of St Frideswide's in Oxford and she was eventually buried there, close to a new chapel which she had paid for. The priory subsequently became Christ Church Cathedral in 1546 and Elizabeth's tomb has survived and is now situated between the Latin Chapel and the Dean's Chapel.[1] William and Elizabeth had four sons, John, William, Simon and Edward. John's early death left as his heir the second son, William, who was born and baptised in 1301 at the chief family home in Cassington, seven miles north-west of Oxford. He probably spent much of his youth either there or at the other main family seat at Yarlington, near Castle Cary in Somerset. When his father died he was aged eighteen and still a minor and as a mark of Edward II's regard for his father he became a ward of the king and was appointed a yeoman of the royal household. The next year, 1320, he accompanied the king and queen on a state visit to France and in 1321 he was granted part custody of his inheritance. However, he was a very young and inexperienced courtier who had little or no influence over the king. Edward's chief advisers by now were the Hugh Despensers, father and son, especially the son.

In 1321 Lancaster and his supporters attacked the lands of the Despensers in the marches and a baronial council dominated by Lancaster found them guilty of breaking the Ordinances of 1311. Lancaster then took control of London and forced the king to exile both Despensers. Edward soon struck back by establishing control over the south-east and south-west and recalling the Despensers from exile. In December he took his army to the Welsh marches, where most of his enemies surrendered, then moved north to confront Lancaster at Burton-on-Trent in March 1322. Lancaster was outnumbered and

The effigy of Elizabeth (née Montford), the wife of William, the second Lord Montagu, on her tomb in Christ Church Cathedral, Oxford. (Robert Douch)

retreated but was brought to battle at Boroughbridge by the king's supporter Andrew Harclay and captured. He was taken to Pontefract Castle where Edward and the young Despenser presided over his trial for treason, at which he was found guilty and sentenced to be hanged, drawn and beheaded. Possibly after a plea for mercy from the queen, he was spared the first two but taken outside the castle and beheaded with two or three blows.[2]

This was Edward's moment of triumph and a wiser ruler would have now behaved with justice and equanimity to restore tranquillity to the kingdom and win back the loyalty of his former opponents. Instead of this and egged on by the Despensers, he embarked upon a concerted campaign of revenge and retribution in which many of his enemies, high and low, were executed and great estates confiscated, while the Despensers pursued personal vendettas, often illegally, were created earls and acquired great wealth and extensive lands. The Ordinances were formally repealed and in 1322 Edward took a large army of some 23,000 men into Scotland but failed to bring Bruce to battle. Andrew Harclay, without the king's authority, suggested to Bruce that he would be recognized as king of Scots in return for a pledge to cease raids on England, only to face Edward's wrath and execution. Even so, a thirteen-year truce with the Scots was subsequently agreed in 1322.

That year, Queen Isabella's brother became King of France as Charles IV and in 1324 he embarked on a determined campaign to assert his overlordship of Gascony. The chief city of Bordeaux was threatened and in 1325 Edward agreed to send his wife to Paris to mediate. Charles IV offered peace if Edward would do homage in person to him for Gascony and Edward agreed but avoided personal involvement by transferring Gascony to Edward, his son and heir. Accordingly, Prince Edward joined his mother in France and performed homage to Charles IV, as required. At this point, Edward expected Isabella and their son to return but they stayed in France, where Isabella had fallen under the influence of the highly ambitious Roger Mortimer, Lord of Wigmore, and both had become sworn enemies of the Despensers, Isabella in particular resenting their influence over her husband.

Isabella agreed a treaty with William, Count of Hainault in the Low Countries, by which Prince Edward would marry his daughter Philippa in return for support in an invasion of England. Isabella and

Mortimer landed in September and immediately found many allies among the barons. Seeing he had lost control over London the king fled westwards with the Despensers and attempted to sail to Ireland, but they were driven back by bad weather to Cardiff and took refuge in Caerphilly Castle. The elder Despenser was captured in Bristol and executed there, while in November, betrayed by his supporters, the king was captured and taken to Kenilworth Castle. In November the young Despenser was found guilty of treason and suffered a disgusting death in Hereford, where he was bound naked to a ladder and castrated and disembowelled while alive, with his genitals and entrails burned in a nearby fire. After this he was beheaded and his body cut into four pieces, while his head was sent for public display and impaled on London Bridge.

On 20 January 1327 the king was informed by a deputation of barons and bishops that if he abdicated his son would be recognized as king but that if he did not, the crown might well be offered to another candidate (Mortimer, for instance). Edward, in despair, agreed, and his son, aged fourteen, was crowned in Westminster Abbey as Edward III on 2 February. By early April the ex-king had been moved to Berkeley Castle, near Bristol, and on 23 September his son was informed that he had died there. Rumours and legends abound concerning the time of his death and how it came about. Some say he was starved to death or suffocated, some that he died of a broken heart; others claim he was murdered by having a red hot iron inserted into his bowels through his anus. An increasing number, led by his biographer Ian Mortimer, argue strongly that he did not die there at all, that Mortimer and Isabella 'faked' his death and that he went abroad to live the life of a hermit in Italy until his natural death about 1342 and that Edward III was well aware of this.[3] What we do know is that, whatever his sexuality might or might not have been, and wherever, whenever or however he died, Edward II while king lacked a truly stunning degree of common sense in showering excessive favours and responsibilities upon two ill-chosen young men, Piers Gaveston and Hugh Despenser, thereby alienating many of those who might otherwise have been his most loyal supporters.

We have little detailed information about the path taken by the third lord Montagu during these perilous times. As a very young man he was in Amiens in 1320 when Edward II performed homage to Philip V of France for Gascony, and he was knighted in 1326[4]. About this time he

The alabaster effigy of Edward II, from his magnificent tomb in Gloucester Cathedral.

married Catherine, the youngest daughter of William, Lord Grandison, and their sons William and John were born in 1328 and 1330. Montagu remained a member of the household of the new king, which suggests that he had not been an overt supporter of the cause of Edward II and was not seen as a threat by Queen Isabella and Roger Mortimer, who now held the reins of power. However unsatisfactory a husband Edward II might have been, it is difficult to applaud Isabella's decision to ally herself with Roger Mortimer, another relative upstart, and to have wilfully launched a rebellion against her husband which resulted in his deposition. For a time, she and Mortimer, created Earl of March, ran the affairs of the kingdom in the name of the young king. They did not run them very well.

In the middle of June 1327 the Scots crossed the border, ending the existing truce, and Roger Mortimer, taking the young king with him, led an army to the North, for which William Montagu was summoned to serve. However, Mortimer was surprised by a night raid at Stanhope, near Durham, in which Edward was nearly captured. This was a major loss of face, but Isabella and Mortimer considered that they did not have the resources to pursue the war, so concluded a treaty signed by Robert Bruce in Edinburgh in March 1328 and ratified by the English Parliament meeting at Northampton in May. In return for £100,000 in cash, Isabella and Mortimer agreed to recognize the kingdom of Scotland as fully independent, to respect the border as it existed in the time of Alexander III and to recognize Robert Bruce as the rightful King of Scots. Moreover, a marriage was agreed between Robert's heir, David, and Edward III's sister Joan. Not surprisingly, this was regarded by most English lords as a disgraceful capitulation and one of those most affronted by it was the young Edward III.

It is likely that from this time onwards the king began to consider how to supplant the authority of his mother and Mortimer and he began to surround himself with loyal friends. In June 1328 William Montagu was advanced to the status of knight banneret and in January 1329 he was granted the manor and castle of Wark, by the river Tweed, in return for contracting to serve the king in peace and war for life with a personal retinue of twenty men-at-arms. Montagu appears as the king's most trusted friend in 1329, accompanying him to France in April that year to render homage to Philip VI at Amiens, and he was in France

A reconstructed image of how Wark Castle in Northumberland (now a ruin) might have appeared in the 14th century.

again in June, trying to conclude marriage treaties with Philip. In September 1329 he was sent to Pope John XXII at Avignon, ostensibly to settle the king's debts but privately to discuss the king's difficult domestic position. The Pope suggested that the king should communicate a private sign to him by which he might know whether or not he was the author of any document and it was agreed that the king would write 'Pater Sancte' on the letter. No doubt as a reward for these diplomatic services, Montagu received further favours and was appointed keeper of the king's stannary and the water at Dartmouth and custodian of Sherborne Castle for life.[5]

The Nottingham coup, October 1330

Roger Mortimer, revelling in the title Earl of March and assured of the affection of Queen Isabella, could not refrain from lavish displays of his new-found wealth and power, such as staging a number of elaborate tournaments on the Arthurian theme. However, he still felt threatened on all sides, as well he might. One of his targets was Edmund, Earl of Kent, the 29-year-old half-brother of Edward II, who was encouraged to believe by Mortimer's agents that the ex-king was still alive and to plot his rescue. Details of Kent's 'treason' were then revealed to the Winchester parliament in March 1330 and he was found guilty and beheaded outside the city, a shocking event that rocked confidence in the Mortimer regime. When Philippa of Hainault provided Edward III with a son and heir in June 1330 Mortimer's position looked even more insecure and he may have begun to consider usurping the throne, especially when it was rumoured that Isabella was carrying his child.

Given these dangers, Edward III and those closest to him realized that the time had come to strike and it is clear that the leader of the king's party was William Montagu. When a council was called to meet at Nottingham Castle in October 1330, Mortimer and Isabella were already in residence there and in possession of the keys, so that when Edward and his court arrived he was told that only he himself with a handful of his retinue would be admitted. According to one chronicler, this affront to the king's dignity led Montagu to advise him that 'it is better to eat the dog than have the dog eat you', and the final straw seems to have been that Mortimer insisted on interrogating the king and his friends, one by one, about a suspected plot. On this occasion it seems that only Montagu was brave enough to answer back that he had done no more than was consistent with his duty to the king.⁶

On the night of 19 October the king, Montagu and his friends, who included Edward Bohun, Robert Ufford, William Clinton and John Neville, gave the appearance of riding away from Nottingham but they returned secretly after nightfall and having previously secured the support of the castle's custodian, William Eland, twenty-four men-at-arms, led by Montagu, made their way by secret passages to Isabella's apartments where they burst in and killed three of Mortimer's guards. Edward kept a cool head during the confusion that followed, while at least one of Mortimer's friends tried to escape via a privy and Mortimer himself hid behind an arras while the queen entreated her son to show mercy.⁷ Mortimer and his son were soon captured, together with their chief supporters, and in a parliament held at Westminster in November Mortimer was found guilty of treason by his peers and hanged at the common gibbet at Tyburn. The king wisely refrained from widespread retribution against Mortimer's friends and continued to treat his mother with consideration and respect. Having just turned eighteen, he emerged from this coup with his reputation much enhanced and with a determination to put a stop to years of English misrule and civil discord, an intention he announced by royal proclamation.

The Westminster parliament encouraged the king to reward William Montagu for his pre-eminent part in the fall of Mortimer and he was granted £1,000 a year for himself and his heirs, together with a grant in tail male of the castle, town, manor and honour of Denbigh in North Wales with the cantreds of Ross, Reywynnock, Kaermer and Dynmael and also the castle of Sherborne in Dorset, valued in all at 1,000 marks. He was also granted the manor and park at Woodstock and the manor of Handborough, both in Oxfordshire.⁸ This generosity compared very favourably with much lesser grants of 400, 300 and 200 marks to Bohun, Ufford, and Neville. According to the chronicler Sir Thomas Gray, for a long time after 1330, 'the king always acted upon the advice of William de Montagu who always encouraged him to excellence and honour and love of arms; and so they led their young lives in pleasant fashion until more serious business came'.⁹

Early in 1331 Edward attempted to negotiate with Philip VI of France over the vexed question of the oaths of homage he was required

Two modern views of the ruins of Denbigh Castle, North Wales, showing what a formidable fortress it would have been in the fourteenth century.

to take for his French possessions. He had performed a vow of homage at Amiens in 1329 but had been careful to leave the terms vague. Philip VI pressed for a more formal vow and threatened consequences if it were not fulfilled. According to the chronicler Geoffrey le Baker, 'the lord king with the bishop of Winchester [John Stratford] and lord William Montagu and just a few others crossed the channel. Just like a merchant, the king travelled with knapsacks but without armour and had barely fifteen horsemen with him. He gave out that he was travelling to fulfil a vow and left his brother John of Eltham in charge of the kingdom.'[10] In fact Edward met Philip in some secrecy at Pont-St-Maxence in April and probably performed homage of a kind, though the details remained unclear and did not, ultimately, resolve the dispute between the two kings.

On the way home from France, the king and Montagu took part in two tournaments, one at Dartford, and one at Cheapside. According to Baker,

> ….a little before the feast of St Michael there were the most handsome tournaments in Cheapside in London, attended by the lady queen Philippa and a large retinue of her maidservants. The canopied tents, which had been newly set up for the spectators of the tournament, collapsed, though without doing any harm. The pious queen did not allow the carpenters to be punished, but by her prayers and genuflexions so recalled the king and his friends from their anger that by this act of mercy she caused everyone to love her, as they thought about her goodness.'[11]

Two ambassadors from Mongolia had visited the court of Edward II in 1307 at Northampton and the king and Montagu hit upon the idea of dressing up for the Cheapside tournament in Tartar dress, while some of the most beautiful women in the land were invited. Decked out in red velvet tunics and white hoods, the colours of St George, they were led by silver chains attached to the right hand of their champion knight.[12] It seems that Montagu was not only the 'captain of these solemnities', but he also footed the very considerable bill for them.[13]

The grant of the Isle of Man, 1333

Robert I of Scotland died in 1329, to be succeeded by his son, David II, aged five, so the kingdom was governed in his name by Thomas Randolph, Earl of Moray and Lord of Man. General dissatisfaction with the treaty of Northampton in England led to renewed demands for war against Scotland, especially among barons, known as 'the disinherited', who had lost possessions as a result of the provisions of the treaty. Chief among these was Henry Beaumont, who persuaded the king to allow him to lead an expedition by sea to Scotland with the support of Edward Balliol, eldest son of John Balliol, who now claimed the Scottish throne. On 20 July 1332 the Earl of Moray died, leaving leadership of the Scottish cause to the Earl of Mar. With much larger forces than the invaders, Mar was overconfident and faced the enemy at Dupplin Moor, near Forteviot, on 11 August, only to be completely outflanked and routed by Beaumont and Balliol, who used a highly successful combination of archers and dismounted men-at-arms. Among those killed in the battle was Thomas Randolph, second Earl of Moray, the son of the first earl, who was now succeeded by his younger brother John Randolph, the third earl. A few weeks later, Edward Balliol was enthroned as king at Scone, opening the way for further English intervention into what had now become another Scottish civil war between the two rival claimants, David II and Balliol.

Edward Balliol's position was shown to be precarious when he was attacked a few months after his enthronement by the Scottish regent Sir Archibald Douglas and the new Earl of Moray and forced to flee to England, where he promised Edward III sovereign control of the lowland counties of Scotland in return for his support. Edward seized this opportunity and moved his court to York, while Balliol and his English supporters besieged Berwick in March 1333. Edward III, at whose command Montagu had raised troops and supplies for the Berwick expedition, arrived at Berwick in person early in May[14]. It was from there on 30 May that, according to Mark Ormrod, Edward 'first announced that Man had been taken into his hands, claiming that his grandfather had been legitimately seized [possessed] of the Island, and, by inference, that the Scottish suzerainty exercised both by John Balliol and latterly by the Bruce monarchy had not been lawful. It is possible that this initial assertion of authority was backed up by a small naval force dispatched to Man from

Bristol in April'. This force appears to have been three warships, under the command of a Roger Turtle, but we cannot be sure from these scraps of information whether this expedition ever sailed to the Island and, if it did, to what extent it managed to chase out the Scots.[15]

By his own calculations, Simon Montagu had 'conquered' the Isle of Man in 1301 and the family's dream of eventually acquiring the lordship began to be realized on 8 June 1333 when Edward committed custody of the Island to Simon's grandson William, his best friend and chief supporter, for fifteen months. Meanwhile, the English attack on Berwick began in earnest and at the end of June its defender, Sir Alexander Seton, requested a truce and was granted one, on condition that he would surrender if not relieved by 11 July. He was also required to provide hostages, including Thomas, the only survivor of his three sons. On the last day of the truce the Scottish army under Archibald Douglas arrived and a detachment under William Keith, after a tussle with Montagu's troops, managed to enter the town and declare that it had been relieved and there would be no surrender.

This infuriated Edward III and he reacted ruthlessly by constructing a high gallows outside the gate of the town where Thomas Seton was hanged in front of his father's eyes, with a promise that the rest of the hostages would follow if there was no surrender. The Scots asked for another truce until 19 July and on that day Douglas's army was ready to fight. Edward had arranged his forces, which included Montagu and his contingent, on the top of the 600-foot high Halidon Hill, two miles to the north-west of Berwick. In order to reach the English, the Scots had to cross marshy ground and then climb the steep hill, and their decision to attack proved disastrous. Douglas and six earls were killed, together with thousands of Scots, while English casualties were slight. Berwick surrendered the following day and Edward II's humiliation at Bannockburn had been avenged.

Very soon after this notable victory Edward III issued letters patent on 9 August which dramatically changed his existing temporary grant of the custodianship of the Isle of Man to William Montagu by recognizing Montagu's 'hereditary and absolute rights to ownership of Man'.[16] According to Mark Ormrod, this 'quitclaim' was 'not a formal transfer of property and rights but a renunciation of Plantagenet claims: the inference was that the [Montagus] had a better right to the Island than had the King of England'.[17] The letters patent were issued in the midst of the tournaments and celebrations marking the capture of Berwick, 'with the assent of the prelates, earls, barons and other nobles present with us', so it was a grant made with the full knowledge of the king's council.[18]

In the absence of any clear evidence that the Isle of Man was firmly under English control at this date, it is reasonable to suggest that this new royal favour to William Montagu was essentially theoretical: indeed, Ormrod makes it clear that Edward III asserted his right to dispose of the Island 'on distinctly tenuous grounds'.[19] For a start, the third Earl of Moray, who survived the slaughter at Halidon Hill, was the undisputed heir of his father the first earl, who had undoubtedly been the de facto Lord of Man from 1316 to 1332. The Island had been under the control of Moray's men for these sixteen years and may well have been still under their control in 1333. Another who had a good claim to Man was Henry Beaumont, who had been granted the Island in such grand terms by Edward II in 1312, but had been dispossessed of it by Robert Bruce the following year. Beaumont was a fierce warrior, the main force behind the 'disinherited' English barons who had made such a success of this Scottish war so far, and it might have seemed sensible for Edward III to have returned the Island to him. Certainly, the Isle of Man would now again be an important strategic factor in the war with Scotland, and Beaumont was the sort of fighter who might be able to capture it from Moray's men and hold it for himself.

On the other hand, the Beaumont grant was tainted because it had been made by Edward II and specifically rejected by the Ordainers. Edward III no doubt granted the Island to Montagu because he was the king's reliable friend, the historical Montagu claim to the Island was very strong, the Montagu family were experienced in warfare at sea and the king felt he could trust Montagu with the ultimate responsibility, first of securing the Island and then of keeping hold of it under a well-organized regime. Even so, it may well be that Montagu was not able to assert his rights over the Island for a considerable time. As we shall see, the chronicler Geoffrey le Baker stated very clearly that Montagu did not 'conquer' the Island and establish himself as the ruler there until nine years later, in 1342. The period from 1333 to 1342 on the Island may well have been one of political and military uncertainty, not least because when Edward III's focus switched in 1337 from warfare in the Irish Sea to conquest in France, the fate of the Isle of Man became less of a priority, both for the king and for William Montagu. However, one reward for Montagu's services at Halidon Hill was more immediate. The original grant of the manor and castle of Wark-on-Tweed for William's lifetime was now extended to his heirs, 'in consideration of the great place which he holds in the affairs of the realm'.[20]

Edward III's natural exuberance and restless energy found release in the extravagant and flamboyant tournaments which he continued to arrange with meticulous detail. A writ of March 1334 ordered the provision of an enormous quantity of elaborate costumes for the participants in the next tournament. These included:

> Three russet coats for the king, William Montagu and John Meules, each coat bearing two figures on the chest each carrying a roll in their hand. A russet coat for the king with a roll above the arms bearing silken letters. Four surcoats of brown scarlet trimmed with miniver for the king, William Montagu, Robert Ufford and Ralph Neville.....A harness for the king for three horses bearing the arms of William Montagu...[21]

The arms in question were a relatively simple design of three red lozenges on a silver background while the family crest (worn on top of the helmet) was a winged griffin.

However, all was not entertainment and Montagu was given important responsibilities. He played a part in the negotiations which followed Halidon Hill and as the titular Lord of Man he was appointed, with others, to be present at the parliament held by Edward Balliol in Edinburgh in February 1334.[22] In May, with David II in exile in France under the protection of King Philip VI, Edward Balliol performed liege homage to Edward III in Newcastle and the English king's administrators were already at work to bring the lowland Scots fully under English control. Montagu, for instance, was one of those who witnessed the letters by which Balliol surrendered lowland towns and castles to the English king.[23]

This apparent triumph did not last because Balliol lacked the support in Scotland necessary to maintain his authority. More than that,

Philip VI effectively announced in 1334 that he would champion the cause of David II, which meant the risk of war with France. That year Montagu accompanied the archbishop of Canterbury, William Clinton and Geoffrey Scrope to France to discuss outstanding issues with Philip VI, which included Scotland, Aquitaine, and the possibility of a joint crusade.[24] In that year, also, Montagu and Henry de Ferrers were appointed keepers of the Channel Islands, for which privilege they paid 500 marks. In return for receiving revenues from the islands they were responsible for their defence from possible French attacks and accordingly they initially appointed Walter de Weston, clerk of the works in the palace of Westminster and the Tower of London, to act as their lieutenant there. Montagu retained responsibility for the islands until 1337.[25]

In June 1335 the king again mustered a large force at Newcastle for a Scottish invasion and for this campaign, Montagu's retinue of 180 men-at-arms, 136 mounted archers and 60 Welsh footmen was the largest single contingent of the army. It was at this time that as a mark of his special esteem, the king granted to Montagu his own personal crest of an eagle, presented him with a charger emblazoned with the Montagu arms and granted him the reversion of five manors totalling £100 a year.[26] The grant of the eagle crest was a sign of exceptional favour but as a gesture of his loyalty and commitment to the royal family Montagu later presented it to the king's baby son, Lionel, when he was asked to act as a godfather to the child in 1338. Meanwhile Edward's army, one of the largest he ever assembled, reached as far as Perth, marching in two columns, but it was unable to defeat the Scottish rebels, now led by Andrew Murray and Robert Steward and bolstered by the moral support of France.[27] The chronicle of Henry Knighton mentions that forces under Montagu's leadership caused much burning, fire and devastation in Scotland. At the close of the campaign Edward, in pursuance of his policy of giving his chief supporters a stake in the domination of Scotland, gave 'his closest friend William Montagu almost independent jurisdiction over a great arc of estates, including the forest of Selkirk and Ettrick and the town and county of Peebles'.[28]

Montagu was among those appointed to negotiate with Andrew Murray but no agreement was reached and in 1336 Edward's spies informed him that the French were planning an invasion of Scotland with a force of 6,000 men in support of their allies.[29] To forestall this a

The seal and counter-seal of William Montagu, describing him (in Latin) as Earl of Salisbury and Lord of Man and Denbigh. (Robert Douch)

modestly-sized English army, this time led by Henry of Grosmont, reached Perth, where he was strengthened by the contingents of several English lords, including Montagu, who was responsible for maintaining control of Stirling Castle through his agents.[30] The king, travelling north with only a few hundred men, joined them in the second half of June and together the combined army embarked on a series of rapid 'scorched earth' attacks, not failing to turn aside to raise the siege of Lochindorb Castle, thereby rescuing a number of beautiful women in the chivalric manner espoused by the king and his close friends.[31] This campaign had the effect of dissuading the French from invading, but the rebel Scots still remained very much at large.

Earl of Salisbury, 1337

On 10 January 1337 Montagu was entrusted with guarding the seas between Portsmouth and Portland and between Portland and Bristol and on the 14th he was appointed 'admiral of the fleet' west of the mouth of the Thames – possibly the first time that this title was used. It carried the responsibility of choosing men to serve in warships and Montagu immediately set about recruiting two thousand archers from the south-west counties.[32]

Soon after this, with the Scottish war far from resolved and the threat of a conflict with France increasingly real, Edward III advanced six of his most trusted supporters to the rank of earl. Many of the existing earls at this time were either elderly or infirm. Thomas of Brotherton, Earl of Norfolk, the king's uncle, was only 37, but he died the following year. Hugh Courtenay, Earl of Devon, was about sixty, Henry of Lancaster was blind and Humphrey Bohun, Earl of Hereford, had an incapacitating illness. To strengthen the nobility and his own support, Edward announced in the Westminster parliament of March 1337 the creation of six new earls. First among them was William Montagu as Earl of Salisbury, followed by William Bohun (Northampton), William Clinton (Huntingdon), Robert Ufford (Suffolk), Henry of Grosmont (Derby) and Hugh Audley (Gloucester). At the same time Edward created his six year-old son and heir not merely an earl but Duke of Cornwall. This was the first creation of a ducal title in England and it showed that Edward III was not going to be outdone by the fancy ducal titles bestowed on the French peerage.[33]

Unlike the favours shown by Edward II to Gaveston, the Despensers and others, the creation of Edward III's new earls caused little resentment. Grosmont and Bohun were in any case closely linked to the royal family, while the others were already of baronial rank. Even so, William Montagu had come a long way since he had helped Edward III to seize power in 1330. The earldom of Salisbury was first created around 1141 for Patrick of Salisbury, a supporter of the Empress Matilda, and it passed to his son William and then to his daughter Ela, who married the famous warrior William 'Longsword', who held the title in right of his wife. Because the rules by which only males could succeed to titles and estates were not formalised until much later, the next holders of the title were both women. The first was William and Ela's only surviving child, Margaret, who married Hugh de Lacy, Earl of Lincoln. The second was their only surviving child, Alice, who, after the death of her parents, became both Countess of Salisbury and Countess of Lincoln in her own right. Edward I ensured she married into the royal family and she became the wife of his nephew Thomas, who already held the earldoms of Lancaster, Leicester and Derby. In fact the marriage was not a success: they lived separate lives and had no children.

After Thomas of Lancaster's execution in 1322 Edward II regarded his lands and titles as forfeit and either took them himself or gave them to his supporters, especially the Despensers. The earldom of Salisbury specifically reverted to the Crown, which explains why it was in the gift of Edward III in 1337: in addition to the title, Montagu was promised lands to the value of 1,000 marks a year.[34] At the time of this great advancement in his career and fortunes Montagu was 36 years old, while his master, the king, was still only 24. As a result of Edward's generosity, Montagu by now owned 27 whole manors, eleven advowsons, five castles and two towns as well as the great and valuable marcher lordship of Denbigh and the more theoretical lordship of Man. The lands he had inherited from his father were worth about £182, but he died worth at least ten times that much.[35]

By 1327 Montagu had married Catherine, the youngest daughter of the first Lord Grandison, and they had six children: two sons, William and John, and four daughters, Elizabeth, Philippa, Sibyl and Agnes. So at this point he was still, by modern standards, a young man with a young family. By 1333 he had lost the sight of one eye, which some said was

An image of the first Earl of Salisbury from the Salisbury Roll, c 1463.

an injury sustained in the Scottish wars, and others a tournament accident.[36] Whether he was tall, short, dark or fair, we do not know, but clearly he was vigorous and energetic, qualities that commended him to the king, and he enjoyed jousting, carousing and taking part in the high-spirited entertainments that were an important part of Edward's lifestyle. Clearly, also, he was loyal and dependable and he gave the king sensible advice. Mark Ormrod considers that 'the two men's habit of exchanging identities and heraldic devices hints that they considered themselves bound by a contract of brotherhood in arms.' Montagu's wife was a friend and confidante of Queen Philippa and received no less than 500 marks from the king when she was able to tell him the good news that his first daughter had been safely born. Indeed, Ormrod is confident that 'the complex and intimate knot of relationships formed by Edward, Philippa, William and Catherine may be said to have become the very centre point of the king's social and emotional existence during the first decade of his majority rule.'[37] Yet whereas in the reign of Edward II the king's favourites had aroused jealousy and hostility among the baronage, this was not the case with Montagu, who was perceived to be worthy of the king's trust and favour.

The start of the 'Hundred Years War', 1337

The creation of the six earls was part of Edward III's newly announced policy of facing up to the threat posed by Philip VI of France, who had allied with the Scots, come close to sending an army to their aid in 1336 and demanded more specific acts of homage from Edward for his French possessions – despite the fact that Edward had already in person performed two such acts in 1329 and 1331. Montagu's first important task as Earl of Salisbury was to accompany the new earls of Northampton and Huntingdon and the Bishop of Lincoln on an embassy in April 1337 to the Duke of Brabant in Brussels and the Emperor Lewis IV in Frankfurt, seeking allies against Philip VI. The ambassadors, magnificently robed and caparisoned, successfully gained the support of a long list of princes, including the counts of Hainault, Gelderland, Berg, Cleves and Julich, the Count Palatine of the Rhine and the Elector of Brandenburg. These all received large payments, but none so great as Duke John of Brabant, who pocketed £60,000.[38] This mission also attempted to negotiate with the French at Valenciennes but Philip VI had made up his mind to attempt to expel the English from France and formally declared war on 30 April, following this with official confiscation of the duchy of Aquitaine and county of Ponthieu.[39] This was no mere formality: the English seneschal in Gascony was required to surrender at once all Edward's towns and castles or face attack by French forces.[40] It can therefore be fairly claimed that it was the King of France who started the conflict which rolled on for more than a hundred years - far longer than he, or anyone else, could have possibly imagined.

Philip VI had come to the throne of France under remarkable circumstances. King Philip IV reigned from 1285 to 1314 and when he died the succession to the throne looked very secure because he left three sons. However, the eldest, Louis X, died after only two years leaving two daughters and a pregnant wife. His younger brother Philip acted as regent until the child was born and it was a son, John I, but he died after a reign of five days in November 1316. Overruling the claims of Louis X's daughters, Philip then effectively usurped the throne as Philip V and called a meeting of the Estates-General in 1317 which confirmed him as king and decreed that women should not succeed to the throne of France.

When he died in 1322 without leaving a son the throne passed to his younger brother Charles IV, who died six years later in 1328, also without a son, the fifth Capetian king to die within 14 years. He left a pregnant queen but before the child was born the principle was again formally laid down that a woman could not succeed to the throne and a number of possible female claimants were specifically excluded, including Isabella, the wife of Edward II, mother of Edward III and sister of the last three kings of France. This time the pregnant queen gave birth to a daughter and the throne passed to the closest male relative of Charles IV who was Philip, Count of Valois, the son of the younger brother of Philip IV. Although a member of the House of Capet, he is nevertheless considered to have begun a new dynasty, the Valois.

Edward III responded to Philip's declaration of war and confiscation of his French lands in October 1337 by laying claim to the throne of France on the grounds that his mother, Isabella, was the sister of Charles IV and he had a more direct claim to the throne through her than Philip of Valois, who was Charles's first cousin. The obvious weakness of his argument was the fact that his claim lay in the female line, while Philip VI was the nearest male heir to Charles IV, had been chosen by the French nobility as king, had been anointed and crowned as such by the church and had been reigning in France without dispute for the last nine years. On the other hand, Philip's confiscation of Aquitaine and Ponthieu was a strongly aggressive move which demanded a vigorous response from Edward if he were not to lose the Plantagenet lands in France. Edward's claim to the throne through Isabella was therefore trumpeted because it gave some degree of legality to his cause.

In an attempt to settle the unrest in Scotland before dealing with France, Salisbury and the Earl of Arundel were appointed joint commanders of a force of about four thousand men which mustered at Newcastle in November and included Genoese carracks and early siege guns.[41] Their aim was to besiege Dunbar, currently the centre of Scottish resistance. The English force arrived outside the walls on 13 January 1338 finding that in the absence of Patrick, Earl of Dunbar, his wife, the dark-haired Agnes, was in command of the garrison. She was the daughter of the first Earl of Moray and the sister of the third earl, who had been ambushed by the English in 1335 and imprisoned in Nottingham Castle. Hence Salisbury, the theoretical Lord of Man, was now attacking the sister of Moray, whose agents may still have been in control of the Island.

Salisbury began by catapulting rocks and lead shot against the walls but this made no impact and the great shield, or 'sow' built to protect his men was crushed by boulders thrown from above. Later he attempted to bribe his way into the castle but was nearly captured when leading a raiding party. He then attempted to starve the defenders but supplies found their way via a postern on the seaward side. Edward III visited the siege in the early stages and later threatened to have his captive, Moray, put to death if his sister continued to defy him.

The siege of Dunbar did not prevent Edward indulging in another of his regular extravagant tournaments, this time held at Havering in March, 1338, where the king and his closest companions were dressed in a blaze of colourful glory. Edward, Salisbury and the Earl of Derby wore tunics of white cloth, trimmed with fur and green cloth, 'decorated with the image of a castle made with silk and trimmed with gold, displaying towers, halls, chambers and other such things, and within the walls divers trees of gold, and on the breasts of each tunic and embroidered figure in gold standing under a canopy on the battlements; the hems of these tunics being designed in such a way as to resemble the moats and ditches of this castle surrounded by a green field'.⁴² By early June it was clear that Dunbar was not going to fall and Edward ordered the unsuccessful besiegers to return to England to take part in his invasion of France. This defeat by a woman (much celebrated as 'Black Agnes' by ballads in Scotland) was quite a humiliation for Salisbury, and Edward's instructions that the siege should be abandoned may have led to the first serious disagreement between himself and the king.⁴³

Even so, within a month Salisbury was sailing with the king and the earls of Northampton, Derby and Suffolk with a force of about 4,000 men to Antwerp, where they joined their Flemish and German allies in the opening moves of what much later historians have conventionally called 'The Hundred Years War'. This is not an accurate description because the last battle is taken as being Castillon in 1453 and peace was not formally made until 1475, long after a hundred years. Moreover, there were decades of peace during this period, which was really a series of separate wars.

Edward III entered the conflict with years of experience gained in his Scottish campaigns and a major personal victory (Halidon Hill) under his belt. His armies were not, as had been the case in previous reigns, summoned through the ancient feudal levies. Jonathan Sumption, the author of a multi-volume history of the Hundred Years War, has this to say about the king's military recruitment methods in his short biography of Edward:

> Apart from a brief experiment in 1346 with conscription according to income, the cavalry who fought in his armies were all volunteers serving with their companies for pay, loot and honour. The same was increasingly true of the archers. Soldiers were recruited by captains who had contracted with the king (or some great lord) to raise a company for his service. They fought together with their friends, neighbours and dependants, sometimes year after year in the same retinues, contributing to the progressive militarization of English society.⁴⁴

In fact it was the Earl of Salisbury who provided the largest personal contingent for this campaign, some 123 men-at-arms and 50 mounted archers and he was later paid £1,238 for the horses which he and his followers lost in the subsequent fighting (his own war horse, or 'destrier' being valued at £60).[45] In addition, he received wages for his men-at-arms and archers, and he was paid for four ships in his possession, 'La Margarete', 'La Cristofre Mountagu', 'La Magdalene Mountagu', and 'La Katerine Mountagu' – names which give a clear indication of how the family chose to spell their surname at this time.[46] In September 1338 Salisbury succeeded the king's uncle, Thomas of Brotherton in the prestigious role of 'marshal of England'.

In Antwerp, Edward III found that his imperial allies were reluctant to march against Philip VI without the authority of the emperor. Hence he journeyed to Koblenz to meet Lewis IV in a showpiece ceremony in the market square, where the alliance was celebrated, and he received the title and crown of 'Vicar-general of the Empire', which gave him imperial authority over all his princely allies. Yet the king was unable to make any further progress for a year, largely because he was very short of money. Moreover, he faced the resolute hostility of Pope Benedict XII who was anxious that Edward should not attack France and should not ally with Lewis IV, who had been excommunicated for supporting an anti-pope. Edward's response was to send a high level embassy to negotiate with Philip, consisting of Salisbury, Richard Bury, the archbishop of Canterbury; Sir Geoffrey Scrope and Bishop Burghersh, though little was achieved and Edward continued with his campaign.[47]

In September 1339 Edward unsuccessfully attacked Cambrai and aided by the Duke of Brabant and the Elector of Brandenburg, he ravaged the countryside round Leon and Soissons. According to the French chronicler Jean le Bel, 'the Earl of Salisbury, the army's marshal, along with the Earl of Suffolk and Sir John of Hainault rode with five hundred men-at-arms to Marle and then fired the suburbs and township of Crécy-sur-Serre and all the surrounding country; they found it richly abundant and looted as they pleased..'[48]

Philip VI and his army came close to the English at Buironfosse but, after much heart-searching, the French decided not to fight and Edward retreated to Brussels. Denied a military success, he could claim the moral high ground because Philip VI had failed to protect his people against death and destruction at the hands of the invaders. In January 1340 Edward secured a diplomatic success by concluding an alliance with the merchant cities of Flanders in return for trading concessions and cash subsidies: they also recognized his claim to the French throne and in a formal ceremony held in Ghent in January, Edward quartered the fleur-de-lys of France with the leopards of England on his arms and thereby assumed a technical dual kingship which was only abandoned by George III in 1802.

Edward had moved his wife and children to Ghent in 1339, during the period of his negotiation with the Netherlands princes, but from time to time he had to return to England and between 17 November 1339 and 11 April 1340, Salisbury was paid five marks a day for the overall responsibility of guarding Queen Philippa and the royal children.[49] But towards the end of April he was unlucky enough to be captured by the French in an incident described in some detail by Geoffrey le Baker:

> Soon after Easter [16 April] the earls of Salisbury and Suffolk with just a few men made an attack on the town of Lille in Flanders which was on the side of the king of France. In pursuing the fleeing Frenchmen they came too close, in fact inside the gates. The portcullis fell. The Englishmen were suddenly surrounded on all sides by a crowd of armed men, taken prisoner and conveyed into France. The two most experienced knights (unless that rash attack should stop them being called experienced) were callously treated by the arrogant and angry Frenchmen. Although they had given their word not to escape when they surrendered, they were actually shackled in irons and carried, not on horseback, but in a cart like robbers. And in the middle of each small town or village an order was given for the cart to halt so that the prisoners could be cursed and shouted at by the populace. Like this they were brought into the presence of the French tyrant, who would have starved them in a squalid prison and then shamefully put them to death, if he had not followed the advice of the king of Bohemia and abstained from his blood lust.[50]

There is more than a hint of reproach in this account that Edward III's right-hand man and marshal of his army should have been so careless as to be captured in what would seem to have been a relative side-show. However, it is extremely unlikely that Philip VI would have contemplating putting these two illustrious captives to death: on the one hand it would have been a gross breach of the rules of chivalry as understood at the time and on the other both were great lords who could be ransomed for very large sums and used as political bargaining-counters. It seems that Salisbury was held in the castle at Montargis, and Suffolk 'in another strong place'.[51]

The capture of Salisbury and Suffolk was undoubtedly a significant blow to Edward III, both in personal terms and as a matter of national morale. Fortunately, in the absence of his marshal, the king pulled off a major victory on 24 June 1340 in a naval encounter between his own fleet of some 160 ships and a larger French force off the Netherlands port of Sluys. It was effectively a battle between ships at very close range and the English were completely victorious. The French fleet was seriously crippled, unable to raid the English south coast as it had done frequently in the preceding years. Moreover, it made the invasion of France in future less of a risk for the English. Edward followed up the victory by unsuccessful land attacks on St Omer and Tournai and challenged Philip VI to a chivalric trial by battle, though without satisfaction. Sensing that his allies were losing enthusiasm and, as ever, short of money, Edward negotiated the Truce of Esplechin in September 1340, to last until midsummer the following year. One of the clauses of this agreement seems to have permitted the release of prisoners taken by both sides and Salisbury was safely back in England six weeks after the truce, though considerable quantities of wool had been sent to Bruges to secure his release. Even so, it seems likely that he was released only in return for a promise that he would not fight in France again, certainly until a sizeable ransom had been paid to Philip VI.[52]

At this point Edward III entered into a bitter dispute with his archbishop of Canterbury, John Stratford, who had been treasurer in the past and whose brother Robert was then the chancellor. The king had persuaded himself that his constant lack of funds was the result of incompetence and corruption among his chief officials, many of whom were arrested, some, such as the wealthy former courtier John Moleyns, by Salisbury.⁵³ Stratford withdrew, Becket-like, to Canterbury, where he assailed the king with strongly written arguments and objections, claiming that royal officials and great lords should not be punished without trial by their peers. On 28 April 1341 a crisis occurred when Stratford was refused access to the parliament chamber in Westminster by Edward's men and a row erupted between him and some of the king's supporters. The Earl of Surrey was brave enough within the chamber to address the king and criticize him for excluding the archbishop and it may be that Salisbury was also among those who encouraged the king to relent. Stratford was allowed in, accompanied by Salisbury and the Earl of Northampton, with Salisbury's brother Simon, Bishop of Ely, carrying the archbishop's cross before him in procession. Once inside the chamber, however, Stratford had to listen to the long list of charges levelled against him by the king.⁵⁴

It seems likely that Salisbury and others now used their influence on the king to bring about a reconciliation with Stratford, which took place on 3 May. Subsequently, a committee consisting of Salisbury and the earls of Arundel, Huntingdon and Suffolk was set up to consider Stratford's objections and they produced recommendations which led to an important statute which laid down that peers of the land and ministers of the king 'should not be arrested or brought to judgement except in parliament and by their peers'.⁵⁵ Edward was eventually persuaded to give up his witch-hunt against Stratford and other officials and it seems clear that Salisbury, while never deserting the king, helped a good deal in persuading him to climb down and abandon his more extreme threats. In due course, much-needed reforms were introduced into the royal financial administration and more revenues flowed in the direction of the king and his military requirements.

Crowned king in the Isle of Man, 1342

In June 1341 David II of Scotland, now aged seventeen, returned to his kingdom from exile in France, took over the reins of government from the guardian, Robert Steward, and made two raids into northern England. This prompted Edward III to march to Newcastle in November and despatch a force which recaptured Stirling castle. He spent Christmas in the North before returning south early in 1342, leaving the Earl of Derby in charge of the negotiation of a truce. After describing Edward's march to Newcastle and campaign against David, the chronicler Geoffrey le Baker crucially goes on to say that after these events:

> William Montagu, Earl of Salisbury, assembled a fleet of small boats and invaded one of the islands (and that the best) of those belonging to Scotland, which are called 'the outer isles'. He was victorious and conquered the whole of this island, which is known as the Isle of Man. The lord king generously gave possession of the island to the earl as its conqueror and had him named and crowned as king of that land.[56]

We know that Salisbury owned several ships and was quite capable of putting together an experienced armed force of knights, men-at-arms and archers in his pay, so there seems no reason to doubt that this was the occasion when he put into effect the grant to him of the lordship of the Isle of Man that Edward III had made back in 1333. Moreover it was a good time to strike, when David II was on the defensive and when the third Earl of Moray, the Scottish claimant to the lordship, was still a prisoner in the Tower of London. In 1342 there were two castles on the Island, Castle Rushen and Peel Castle, of which Castle Rushen was the more impressive fortification, though it had been badly damaged over the years. It is not likely that either it or Peel Castle would have been sufficiently well defended to hold out against the seasoned troops of Salisbury, who was already himself an experienced campaigner.

The most intriguing of Baker's statements is that Salisbury was 'crowned king of that land'. Baker was more or less a contemporary of Salisbury so this statement is powerful evidence that the Island's ancient status as a kingdom outside the immediate control of either England or Scotland was still recognized, not only on the Island itself, but beyond. There seems to be no existing evidence that Salisbury, or his son, used the title of King of Man outside the Island during their lifetimes: surviving English documents and charters show that they styled themselves Earl of Salisbury and Lord of Man. However, no documents or charters pertaining to the internal affairs of the Isle of Man have survived from the Montagu period, and it is quite possible that they might have been accorded the title of 'King' within the Island. Certainly, the Manx tradition of kingly status persisted and even increased under the successors of the Montagus.

We do not know any details of the military or governmental regime that Salisbury established on the Isle of Man after he had taken possession of it. One reason for this is that 'The Chronicles of the Kings of Man and the Isles', the main source for the Island's history from about 1000 AD, restricts itself after 1316 only to short biographical accounts of the bishops of Man. Secondly, because Edward III formally renounced his royal rights in the Island in 1333, its records were not kept in the English governmental archives. A further reason is that the records of the earls of Salisbury, which would presumably have retained documents and charters relevant to the Island up to the 1390s, have subsequently been lost or destroyed.

Clearly the full acquisition of the lordship and titular kingship of Man was a major feather in the cap of the Earl of Salisbury. During Bishop Bek's time he paid the king 1,000 marks a year and Bek maintained a military custodian at Castle Rushen as well as a civilian administrator who was responsible for the collection of the rents and dues owed to the lord. During the Moray lordship these posts would have been filled by Scotsmen while under Salisbury the officials would have been men loyal to himself. The Island was also important geographically as a staging-post in the Irish Sea and as a bulwark against future Scottish incursions. For this reason it is possible that Salisbury took steps to strengthen the fortifications of Castle Rushen, perhaps drawing on his experience as lord of Wark and Denbigh, which both boasted impressive castles.[57]

Some thirty miles long by fifteen wide, the Island in 1342 probably had a population of only a few thousand people who lived in homesteads based upon 700 or so quarterland farms. Houses were of the Norse, rectangular type and generally small while two languages were probably still in use, the original Gaelic and Norse – because many Viking warriors had married local girls. Most islanders made their livelihood from farming or fishing and there were no towns or even villages. Nor were there baronial castles or manor houses because feudalism had not been introduced to the Island, though there were two castles built by the earlier kings – one on St Patrick's Isle at Peel, and one at Castle Rushen. The Island was an ancient Christian community in which about seventeen parishes had been established by 1200, each with

Diagram of 14th century locations on the Isle of Man.

a parish church and some smaller 'keeills', or chapels. A bishop of Man had existed since very early times and there was a cathedral on St Patrick's Isle in Peel, as well as a small Cistercian abbey at Rushen.

The most distinctive feature of the Isle of Man and the main reason why it continued to be treated as a 'special case' by other rulers, was its ancient Scandinavian form of government. By the late tenth century 'Tynwald' was established as a sort of parliament at which the chief freemen of the Island, later known as 'the Keys', advised the king or lord concerning the promulgation of new laws and the interpretation of old customs and there was a strong tradition of local consultation. This alone marked it out as a very different lordship from those held directly from the crown in England or Scotland.

Campaigns in Brittany, 1343

Regarding his ongoing contest with Philip VI, Edward suffered two blows in the summer of 1341. One was the decision of the Emperor Lewis to withdraw from his alliance with Edward and to deprive him of the title of vicar-general. The second blow was the election of Philip VI's close adviser Pierre Roger, as Pope Clement VI. Edward needed new allies in France and decided to make use of a conflict that had developed over the succession to the dukedom of Brittany. Duke John III died in April 1341, leaving his title in dispute between two relatives, Charles of Blois and John de Montfort. Philip VI supported Charles of Blois and held Montfort prisoner, so in 1342 Edward III determined to back Montfort, whose adherents, especially his attractive wife, in return recognized Edward's claim to be the rightful king of France.

After his return from Scotland in 1342 the king held an impressive round of tournaments at Dunstable, Northampton and Eltham to encourage the spirit of arms among his knights and major meetings of the council took place at Westminster in April and Woodstock in June. It is likely that Salisbury, his conquest of the Isle of Man assured, was present at many of these events: he certainly attended a great banquet held at Eastry in September, hosted by the king and queen, and attended by the young Prince of Wales and the earls of Derby, Warwick and Suffolk. As part of his preparations for a campaign in Brittany Edward negotiated with Philip VI for the release of Salisbury from his promise not to fight again in France. This was achieved in return for the release of Edward's prisoners, the Scottish Earl of Moray and the Breton lord, Hervé de Leon. It is also probable that at least part of the ransom for Salisbury was paid by the king in return for the cancellation of a sum of £6,700 owed by Edward to Salisbury for war service. Whether part of the deal for Moray's release included his acceptance of the loss of the Isle of Man is impossible to say.[58]

In October Edward's fleet left the ports of Sandwich and Winchelsea and sailed to Brittany, arriving in Brest after a stormy crossing. A force under Northampton defeated the French at Morlaix, while Edward's main army marched south to besiege the port of Vannes late in November. The garrison held firm, so raiding parties under Salisbury, Northampton and Warwick fanned out across Brittany, with Salisbury devastating the town of Dinan. Faced with this, Pope Clement brokered the truce of Malestroit on 19 January 1343, designed to last for three years and six months. This provided terms favourable to the English: the release of John of Montfort from prison and the grant of all territory captured by the English except for Vannes, which was placed under papal control. Edward III and his army arrived back in England in March 1343 and the king decided that he would not initiate another campaign against David II of Scotland, who had managed to secure control of Stirling and Roxburgh while Edward had been on campaign in Brittany. Accordingly a truce with Scotland was agreed in June 1343 to last for three years.

The king then sent Salisbury and the Earl of Derby on a mission which was to some extent a crusade. Since attaining his majority in 1325, Alfonso XI, King of Castile, Leon and Galicia, had embarked upon a ruthless policy of establishing his royal authority within his own dominions and then of attacking the Moslem rulers of nearby Gibraltar and Algeciras, as part of the long-running 'Reconquista' campaigns of Spain's Christian kings to drive the Moslems from the Iberian peninsula. Alfonso captured Gibraltar in 1340 and then struck against the bigger prize of Algeciras, which he began to besiege in the summer of 1342 with the help of a Portuguese army and a Genoese fleet. The first attacks floundered, especially after the Moslem emirate of Granada sent troops to assist in the defence of the city and Alfonso then appealed for international help, supported by Pope Clement VI. In response to this the king of Navarre took an army in person, Philip VI of France sent a detachment under the Count of Foix and Edward III sent Salisbury and the Earl of Derby as part of an embassy which arrived in May 1343. Both earls played some part in the siege of Algeciras and acquitted themselves well in addition to negotiating a marriage alliance between Alfonso's son and heir and Edward's daughter Joan.[59] Algeciras eventually surrendered to Alfonso XI in March, 1344.

The Feast of the Round Table and Salisbury's death, January 1344

Salisbury returned to England late in 1343, possibly having contracted an illness of some sort in Spain, according to the Spanish chronicler Nunez de Villasan, but he was well enough to take part in an exceptional event which the king held at Windsor Castle in January 1344.[60] This was the so-called 'Feast of the Round Table', no doubt mainly intended as a recruitment drive for the next stage in Edward's contest with Philip of France. Adam Murimuth, a canon of St Paul's Cathedral, has left a contemporary account of what took place:

> In this year the lord king ordered a most noble tournament or joust to be held in his birthplace, that is at Windsor Castle, on January 19, which he caused to be announced a suitable time in advance both abroad and in England. He sent invitations to all the ladies of the southern part of England and to the wives of the citizens of London. When the earls, barons, knights and a great number of ladies had gathered on the Sunday, January 19, the king gave a solemn feast, and the great hall of the castle was filled by the ladies, with just two knights among them, the only ones to have come from France for the occasion. At this gathering there were two queens, nine countesses, the wives of the barons, knights and citizens, whom they could not easily count, and to whom the king himself personally allocated their seats according to their rank. The Prince of Wales, Duke of Cornwall, earls, barons and knights ate with all the other people in tents and other places, where food and all other necessities had been prepared: everything was on a generous scale and served unstintingly. In the evening,

The Mighty Montagus

dancing and various entertainments were laid on in magnificent fashion. For the three days following, the king with nineteen other knights held jousts against all comers; and the king himself, not because of his kingly rank but because of his great exertions and the good fortune that he had during the three days, was held to be the best of the defenders.[61]

The jousting lasted from Monday to Wednesday, and according to Murimuth:

That night, after the end of the jousts, the king had it proclaimed that no lord or lady should presume to depart, but should stay until morning, to learn the king's pleasure. When the morning of Thursday came, at about nine o'clock the king caused himself to be solemnly arrayed in his most royal and festive attire; his outer mantle was of very precious velvet and the royal crown was placed upon his head. The queen was likewise dressed in most noble fashion. The earls and barons, and the rest of the lords and ladies, prepared themselves in appropriate fashion to go with the king to the chapel in the castle of Windsor and hear Mass, as he commanded them to do. When Mass had been celebrated, the king left the chapel; Henry, Earl of Derby, as steward of England, and William, Earl of Salisbury, as marshal of England, went before him, each carrying the staff of office in his hand, and the king himself holding the royal sceptre in his hand...... The king was presented with the Bible, and laying his hand on the Gospels, swore a solemn oath that he himself at a certain time, provided that he had the necessary means, would begin a Round Table, in the same manner and conditions as Arthur, formerly king of England, established it, namely to the number of 300 knights, and would cherish it and maintain it according to his power, always adding to the number of knights. The earls of Derby, Salisbury, Warwick, Arundel, Pembroke and Suffolk, the other barons and very many praiseworthy knights of probity and renown likewise made an oath to observe, sustain, and promote the Round Table with all its appendages. When this was done, trumpets and drums sounded together, and the guests hastened to a feast, where richness of fare, variety of dishes, and overflowing abundance of drinks were all to be found, to their unutterable delight and inestimable comfort.[62]

This celebration feast took place on Thursday, 24 January but six days later, on the 30th, the Earl of Salisbury died. Whether this was the result of the illness he had contracted in Spain or of complications from a wound suffered during the Windsor jousts, or both, is not clear.[63] He was 42 years old and he had been the king's closest friend and supporter since 1330 at least, and his death came as a nasty shock. The court went into mourning and Edward III attended a special memorial Mass at St Paul's Cathedral on 4 February, after which Salisbury's remains were interred at Bisham Priory. In 1333 Edward had granted Montagu the reversion to the manor of Bisham, bordering the river Thames in Berkshire. As well as extensive surrounding lands the manor included a substantial house which had been built as a preceptory (or administrative centre) by the Knights Templar around 1260. The order was suppressed in 1307 and the manor reverted to Edward II who used the house as a place of detention for several notables, including the wife of Robert Bruce. In April 1336 Montagu obtained a licence from the king to found a house of Augustinian canons there - a religious community under less strict discipline than monks. He also obtained permission to build a priory church for them close to the existing building and to endow it with lands, rents and advowsons worth £500 a year. Thomas Wiltshire was appointed the first prior in 1337 and the income of several manors was set aside as an endowment. It was Montagu's intention from the outset that the new priory should be a suitable resting place for himself and his successors and the foundation stone was laid by no less a person than the king himself, as recorded by an existing inscription (in French) which translates as 'Edward, King of England who set the siege before the city of Berwick and won the battle there at the said city on the eve of St Margaret in the year of grace mcccxxxiii laid this stone at the request of Sir William de

Montagu founder of this house…'.⁶⁴ In 1340 Salisbury was also granted custody of the old-established priory of Montacute in Somerset, together with its dependent cells in Dorset, Cornwall and Devon.⁶⁵

Some historians have argued that Edward III was over-generous to Salisbury. G.A.Holmes wrote that 'the lifetime of the first earl [of Salisbury] is perhaps the most conspicuous case in the fourteenth century of a sudden rise to greatness through royal favour and patronage', while K.B.McFarlane criticised the king's 'too liberal endowment' of Salisbury and felt that it set a bad example.⁶⁶ The king was certainly generous. In addition to his earldom and the rank of marshal of the army, between 1330 and his death Salisbury received from the king lands to the value of at least £1,400 a year in addition to the reversions of many properties, wardships of minors and grants of the custody of royal castles and manors, all of which generated revenues. In addition he owned estates in Scotland and Ireland, the island of Lundy and the Isle of Man. Moroever, Salisbury's possessions ranged widely across England with, apart from the western estates, major concentrations round the lordship of Denbigh in North Wales, in East Anglia, and the 'home counties', as well as estates in Peebles, Selkirk and Wark in the far North.

It was not only the earl himself who benefited from the king's generosity. He had two younger brothers, Simon and Edward, as well as six sisters. Simon became a priest and as early as 1329 Edward III nominated him as archdeacon of Wells, though this was contested by other candidates. He became archdeacon of Canterbury in 1332 and in the same year he was the king's candidate for the rich bishopric of Winchester, though the Pope intervened and managed to secure the election of Adam Orleton, bishop of Worcester. So Simon took Orleton's place as bishop of Worcester in 1334, when he was aged about 30, and in 1337, this time with papal approval, he was translated to the richer see of Ely, where he remained until his death in 1345, only one year after his brother.

Salisbury's other brother, Edward, born around 1315, was knighted in 1337 and granted an annuity of £100 by the king. In 1338 he contracted a highly prestigious royal marriage with Alice, the daughter and co-heiress of Thomas of Brotherton, Earl of Norfolk, a son of Edward I and uncle of the king. Edward served in the Low Countries in 1338 and as part of Salisbury's contingent in Brittany from 1343. As for Salisbury's six sisters, the eldest three married West Country knights, while the

Bisham Abbey from the air, mid-twentieth century.

The Templars' Great Hall in Bisham Abbey.

youngest three became nuns and eventually abbesses. As for Salisbury's own children by his wife, Catherine Grandison, his two sons and four daughters all married into the highest circles of society. At the age of 13, in 1341, the eldest son, William, was contracted to marry Joan of Kent, a member of the royal family, while the younger son, John, was married to Salisbury's ward Margaret, the heiress of Thomas de Monthermer. Of the daughters, Elizabeth was married three times - to Giles Badlesmere, Hugh Despenser and Guy de Bryan, Philippa married Roger Mortimer, the second Earl of March, Sibyl married a son of the Earl of Arundel and Agnes married Lord Grey de Ruthin.[67]

What did Edward III get in return for his unstinted support of his friend William Montagu and his family? For a start, the two were friends even before the 'coup' of 1330 and this implies a mutual compatibility and understanding, despite the age difference of some eight years. Mark Ormrod suggests that the king, as the product of a dysfunctional family, appreciated Montagu as an 'older brother figure', or brother-in-arms, having only one blood brother, John of Eltham, who was four years his junior and who died aged twenty in 1336, in addition to two younger sisters.[68]

There can be no doubt at all that Montagu gave the teenage king vital support in the Nottingham coup of 1330 and led the young men who toppled Mortimer from power, and that was the main reason why he received rewards worth at least £1,000 a year - chiefly Mortimer's lordship of Denbigh - soon afterwards. The fact that a strong friendship between Montagu and the king persisted from 1330 to his death shows that trust remained unshaken on both sides. Certainly one of the king's great qualities was his ability to 'get on' with people and to inspire loyalty and respect among his friends, while Montagu gave the king no cause to regret the friendship. As we have seen, he was the first to support Edward in all his endeavours, whether military, diplomatic or political, and as Earl of Salisbury he also gave the often impecunious king a great deal of financial support – to such an extent that when he died the king was considerably in debt to him. Yet most of the gifts of land Montagu received were made, not from the royal estate, but from the lands of Roger Mortimer and others who were disinherited for one reason or another. The grant of the Isle of Man, moreover, because of its unique status, cost the king very little in financial terms. So, given the loyal support which Edward III received from William Montagu from 1330 to 1344, as outlined in the pages above, it is surely the case that, far from being too generous, Edward III received a notable bargain.

Did Edward III rape Salisbury's wife?

Edward III married Philippa of Hainault in January 1328, when she was thirteen and he was fifteen. Though an arranged marriage, it was a very happy one and it produced thirteen children. William Montagu married Catherine Grandison a few months earlier when he was 26 and she was about 23, and they had six children. Although both men were enthusiastic exponents of the 'art of chivalry', which involved the admiration of courtly ladies and a degree of formal dalliance with them, neither of them up to 1342 had a public reputation for adultery, and both were firm friends. Moreover, given that they had both been married for the best part of twelve years, it would seem impossible that Edward III had not met Catherine Montagu countless times during that period on state and court occasions and at tournaments.

Yet the Hainault chronicler Jean le Bel, writing about fifteen years after the events he alleged, accused Edward III of no less than the brutal rape of the Countess of Salisbury, describing his villainy in unnerving detail. The main ingredients of le Bel's story are that in the winter of 1341-2 Edward visited an unspecified castle in the north of England which belonged to Salisbury and where his wife (whom he incorrectly calls Alice) was resident while he was a prisoner in France. The king was so impressed by the beauty of the countess that he summoned Salisbury (by then released) and his wife to a great tournament in London in August 1342, in order to see more of her. Then the king sends Salisbury away on campaign to Brittany and pretending to inspect his lands in the North he returns to the castle and then, according to Le Bel:

> …..he entered the lady's chamber, then shut the doors of the wardrobe so that her maids could not help her, then he took her and gagged her mouth so firmly that she could not cry out more than two or three times, and then he raped her so savagely that never was a woman so badly treated; and he left her lying there all battered

The Mighty Montagus

about, bleeding from the nose and mouth and elsewhere, which was for her great damage and great pity.[69]

According to Le Bel, the countess subsequently confessed her rape to her husband, who confronted the king. Edward III's response was to order him to give up his properties and go on crusade, where he died fighting against the Moslems. But Salisbury did not die fighting the Moslems, nor did he make any arrangements to dispose of his properties and there are so many other inaccuracies and improbabilities in this story that it would seem difficult to take it at all seriously. The famous chronicler Jean Froissart, who knew Edward III personally, used le Bel's chronicle as the basis for the early parts of his own work and was deeply shocked, it seems, when he read about the rape accusation. In an early version of his own chronicle he wrote this:

> ...Jean le Bel relates in his chronicle that the English king raped the Countess of Salisbury. Now I declare that I know England well, where I have lived for long periods mainly at the royal court and also with the great lords of the country. And I have never heard tell of this rape although I have asked people about it who must have known if it had ever happened. Moreover, I cannot believe it and it is incredible that so great and valiant a man as the King of England would have allowed himself to dishonour one of the most notable of ladies of his realm and one of his knights who had served him so loyally all his life.[70]

The rape of the Countess of Salisbury, along with many other vivid stories such as the red-hot poker details concerning Edward II and the murder by Richard III of the princes in the Tower, has become one of the main talking-points of medieval English history, and it was certainly very well known when it first circulated in Europe in the late 1350s. Some aspects of the story are plausible – Edward would have passed by Wark Castle during his march up to Newcastle and into Scotland in the winter of 1341-2, and there was a great tournament in London in the summer of 1342 to mark the wedding of the king's son, Lionel. But, as we have seen, Salisbury was not a prisoner in France at the time of the alleged rape – he was captured in April 1340 and released on parole a few weeks after the Truce of Esplechin in September that year. So any suggestion that his wife was left without the protection of her husband in the winter of 1341-2 cannot be correct. Exhaustive scholarly enquiries into the story by Antonia Gransden in 1972 and Ian Mortimer in 2007 have come to the conclusion that it flies in the face of all likelihood. They argue that Jean le Bel probably picked it up from scurrilous French sources whose purpose was to discredit Edward III and his claim to be the rightful king of France by portraying him as the blackest of villains, treacherous even to his closest friend and guilty of the rape of a high-born lady, the very antithesis of the code of honour held in such high regard at the time.[71]

But there is another faint possibility. Michael Packe, in his biography of Edward III, published in 1983, gave a great deal of attention to the rape story and came to the conclusion that the Montagu whose wife was raped was the earl's younger brother, Edward. He was indeed the castellan of the earl's castle of Wark and his wife was called Alice. She was a cousin of the king, being the daughter of Thomas of Brotherton, a younger brother of Edward II, and she had married Montagu around 1337, when she was twenty years junior to her husband. Packe argues that it was Alice whom the king met at Wark and that she accompanied her husband to a meeting of the Great Council in London the following year. Montagu was then sent on a military mission to Brittany, leaving Alice at their family home, Bungay Castle in Suffolk, where the king secretly visited and assaulted her.

Of course, Montagu was not subsequently told to relinquish his properties, nor did he die on crusade against the Moslems: he was fit and well enough to be summoned to parliament as a baron in 1348. Even so, Packe goes on to claim that according to 'incontrovertible public records', which unfortunately he does not cite, Alice was eventually murdered by her husband in 1351, battered to death in a rage. The king did not punish him for this outrage against a member of the royal family and indeed prevented criminal proceedings from taking place, and Packe suspects this is because Montagu knew that the king had raped his wife.[72]

William Montagu, second Earl of Salisbury, 1328-1397

Crécy and Calais, 1346-1347

The first Earl of Salisbury had two sons, William, born on 28 June 1328 at his manor of Donyatt in Somerset and John, born in 1330. As a boy William was raised with his brother in the company of other distinguished youngsters such as Edward, the Prince of Wales, born in 1330, and also Joan, born in 1328, daughter of the Edmund, Earl of Kent, who had been executed by Isabella and Mortimer for treason in 1330. Kent left a widow and four children, all of whom were taken under the protection of the young Edward III after the fall of Mortimer. In 1341 the king, as a sign of his continued favour, gave permission for a marriage to be contracted between Salisbury's elder son and Joan of Kent, both then aged thirteen, which meant that the Montagus had risen so far as to be acceptable marriage partners for the royal family. When his father died in 1344 William was only sixteen, so he became a ward of the king who thereby became ultimately responsible for the young earl and his countess and all their possessions until William reached the age of twenty-one. For day-to-day supervision of the young earl and his affairs, the king appointed Sir John Wingfield as his guardian.

In 1345 Edward III renewed his offensive against France with a three-pronged campaign. One army under Derby (who became Earl of Lancaster on the death of his father during this year) was sent to Aquitaine and another under Northampton to Brittany, while the king himself went again to Flanders, largely to re-negotiate his treaties with the Flemish towns. Lancaster was successful in a number of engagements where many notable prisoners were taken, resulting in profitable ransoms and a good deal of plunder, though Northampton achieved little of significance. In the following year, 1346, Edward's fortunes turned spectacularly. Godfrey de Harcourt, a Norman baron, appealed to Edward as the rightful king of France to come to his aid in a dispute with Philip VI and Edward used this excuse to cross to Normandy with an army of

Kings of France
Philip IV	*1285 ~ 1314*
Louis X	*1314 ~ 1316*
John I	*1316 ~ 1316*
Philip V	*1316 ~ 1322*
Charles IV	*1322 ~ 1328*
Philip VI	*1328 ~ 1350*
John II	*1350 ~ 1364*
Charles V	*1364 ~ 1380*
Charles VI	*1380 ~ 1422*
Charles VII	*1422 ~ 1461*

Kings of England
Edward II	*1307 ~ 1327*
Edward III	*1327 ~ 1377*
Richard II	*1377 ~ 1399*
Henry IV	*1399 ~ 1413*
Henry V	*1413 ~ 1422*
Henry VI	*1422 ~ 1461*

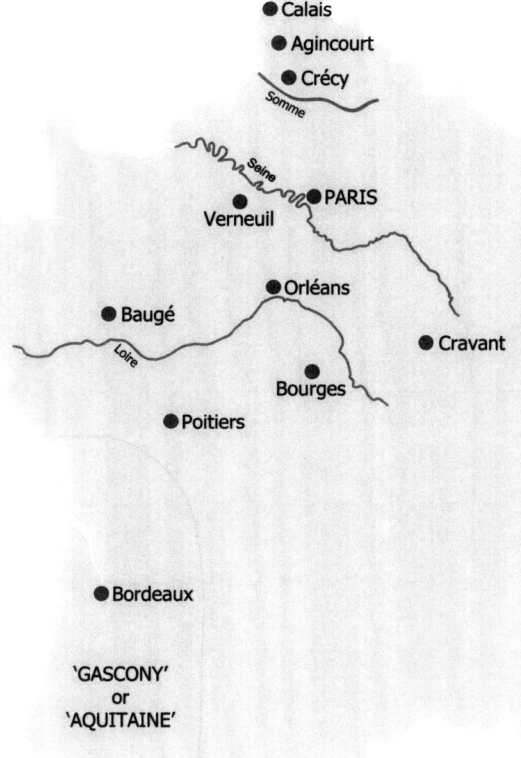

Diagram of France showing important locations in the Hundred Years War.

15,000 men, which included the young Earl of Salisbury. On landing at La Hogue on 12 July, Edward lost no time in seeking out a convenient small hill where he knighted his eldest son, the Prince of Wales, along with the prince's boyhood friends the young Earl of Salisbury and Roger Mortimer, grandson of the executed first Earl of March, who was gradually winning back the confidence of the king.[1]

Edward's first major success was the capture of Carentan and then the well-defended town of Caen, which resulted in the taking of valuable prisoners and looting on a grand scale. After this his army marched along the Seine and by 13 August was only fifteen miles from Paris, the Valois capital. Philip at this point signalled his intention to give battle and seeking a favourable location for the contest, Edward took his army north and crossed the Somme at Blanchetaque. On August 26 he drew up his army of up to 15,000 men on a ridge near the village of Crécy and faced Philip VI, who had a force about ten thousand stronger, including Genoese crossbowmen.

As rain began to fall in the late afternoon, the French attacked but were immediately hit by a storm of arrows from the English longbows. Philip's brother the Duke of Alençon led a misguided cavalry charge which reached the Prince of Wales but suffered heavy casualties. Edward watched the battle from a hilltop windmill, but his son remained in the thick of the action, 'winning his spurs', though he was lucky not to be captured. Nightfall ended the fighting and in the morning the battlefield was seen to be piled high with the fallen French. Among the most notable was Philip's ally the blind King of Bohemia, one duke, six counts and many lesser lords. Between 1,500 and 2,000 French men-at-arms were killed and an unknown number of archers and infantry. The official score of dead English knights and esquires was 350. The Earl of Salisbury, fighting in the king's division, was among the many who survived unharmed.[2]

This spectacular success, which transformed Edward's reputation as a warrior king, was followed by his immediate decision to lay siege to the port of Calais, where he arrived on 3 September. Meanwhile, David II of Scotland used the absence of Edward to invade north-eastern England in October with about 12,000 men. The Scots were confronted on 17 October by about 6,000 English forces led by the archbishop of York at Neville's Cross, outside Durham, and suffered a

An eighteenth century engraving of the surrender of Calais in August 1347 to Edward III, with Queen Philippa on her knees begging for the lives of the town's leading citizens. By Edward Hall, 1776. Courtesy of the National Portrait Gallery.

severe defeat after three hours of fighting. Five Scottish earls were killed, including the Earl of Moray, while David II himself was taken prisoner after suffering arrow wounds to the face. Edward ordered that he should be treated with great courtesy, as an honoured guest, but he was a prisoner all the same.

While Edward continued to besiege Calais the Earl of Lancaster attacked Poitiers and plundered the surrounding region, which deflected Philip VI's attention from the relief of Calais. The English army experienced hard conditions outside the walls of the city during the winter of 1346-7, with cold and dysentery constant problems, but reinforcements from England brought the numbers up to about 26,000 men, accommodated in a vast temporary town outside the walls. The king and the royal family established themselves there, as did most members of the aristocracy - keen to have a role in the expected surrender. In Mark Ormrod's view, 'With hundreds of knights and esquires gathering in the retinues of these great lords, the siege of Calais turned into one of the greatest gatherings of chivalry known in the later Middle Ages'.[3] Salisbury was certainly with the king at Calais, and probably his countess, Joan, as well.

The siege dragged on because the English were unable to breach or scale the walls or to enforce a complete blockade, though supplies ran very low within the town. Late in July 1347 Philip arrived in the Calais region with a large army but failed to persuade Edward either to negotiate a settlement or fight a battle at a place of Philip's choosing. Philip then effectively abandoned Calais, which had no choice but to surrender on 3 August. Six of its leading townsmen famously delivered the keys to the king with nooses round their necks to indicate their recognition of the fact that, according to the rules of war accepted at the time, not only they but all the citizens had forfeited their lives and possessions. Froissart claims that Queen Philippa successfully begged for clemency, which her husband graciously granted, further enhancing his reputation as a great, but merciful, conqueror.[4]

Whereas Edward's reign up to 1346 had generally been one of unfulfilled promise in his Scottish and French campaigns and had also been marred by the conflict with archbishop Stratford in 1340-1 as well as widespread resentment at his constant demand for money through excessive taxation, the rush of outstanding successes at Crécy, Neville's

Cross and Calais silenced Edward's critics and allowed him to bask for the next twenty years at least in his reputation as the most successful and respected warrior king in Europe.

The Garter, plague, and 'divorce', 1347-1349

Unfortunately, the Earl of Salisbury was not able to join wholeheartedly in the celebrations after the fall of Calais because he learned, about this time, the very unwelcome news that someone else was claiming to be the lawful husband of his wife, Joan of Kent. This was Sir Thomas Holland, from a Lancashire knightly family, who had been steward of William's household before fighting in Flanders in 1340 and then in France in 1342 and 1343. He was part of Edward III's army that attacked Caen on 25 July 1346 and was lucky enough to be the man to whom the Count of Eu, the city's main defender and the constable of France, surrendered on that day. Holland subsequently sold the count and his ransom to Edward III for the huge sum of £12,000 and thus enriched he felt able to announce that he had made a secret marriage with Joan of Kent in 1340, before leaving for Flanders. Joan had later succumbed to family pressures and agreed to marry William Montagu in 1341, saying nothing about the Holland marriage because it had taken place without the king's consent, and she was under his protection. She was, in addition, a child of twelve at that time, while Holland was 26 years old.

Salisbury was horrified at this news, which threatened to deprive him of his young wife of royal status who was already being hailed as one of the most beautiful and alluring women of the age. Sir Thomas Holland evidently thought she was because he made use of his ransom money to bring his case before the papal court in Avignon, seeking an annulment of the Salisbury marriage. Edward III decreed that Joan should say whether the Holland marriage had taken place or not, and she admitted that it had. Furious at this decision, Salisbury allegedly confined her within their own home, while the papal decision was awaited.

The king arrived back in England early in October 1347 and spent most of the next nine months celebrating the Christmas and New Year festivities and presiding over tournaments held in Reading, Bury St Edmund's, Lichfield, Eltham, Windsor and Canterbury, where he and his courtiers often dressed in fantastic costumes and enjoyed flamboyant displays. It was after the Windsor tournament, in late June, that Edward put into effect his revised scheme for an order of élite chivalric knights, which had first surfaced in 1344 at the 'Round Table' festival. As it emerged in 1348 the new order, with its symbol of a military garter similar to those worn by knights and its cloak of dark blue, was to be restricted to 26 men personally chosen by the king. The intention was probably to commemorate the battle of Crécy and it is significant that all but two of the knights originally chosen had fought in that battle or related campaigns. The knights would be divided into two teams of twelve for jousts and tournaments, with the king in charge of one team and the Prince of Wales the other. In August Edward founded what would eventually be the magnificent gothic chapel of St George at Windsor, which was to be the new order's spiritual home.[5]

Among the founding knights, there were only three earls, Lancaster, Warwick and Salisbury, in addition to a handful of barons. The rest were knights of lesser renown and they included Sir Thomas Holland and his younger brother, Sir Otes. Clearly, the founding knights were chosen not simply because of their established place in the aristocratic or social hierarchy, but because of the regard the king had for their service during the Crécy campaign. The fact that Salisbury was included with the renowned commanders Lancaster and Warwick must therefore be a significant sign that at this stage, despite his youth, he had succeeded in making a very good impression. He was probably not too pleased, however, with the inclusion of the Holland brothers.

The long-enduring legend, which did not develop until Tudor times, that the garter was chosen as an emblem because it was a lady's garter that Edward III picked up at a ball where it had been dropped by 'the Countess of Salisbury' has generally been discounted by recent historians. The two chroniclers considered most responsible for this misunderstanding are Jean Froissart who confused the 1344 Round Table festival with the later foundation of the order, and Jean le Bel who produced the dubious story of Edward's rape of a Countess of Salisbury. The order's motto, 'Honi soit qui mal y pense' (Shame on those who think ill of it) therefore in all likelihood refers to Edward's claim to the throne of France, not any alleged love affair with a Countess of Salisbury, as later commentators, including the author of the 'Shakespeare' play, 'Edward III', would have us believe.[6]

The rejoicing and jollification at Edward's court in the summer of 1348 was drastically overshadowed in the second half of the year by the arrival on English shores of what has since been called the 'Black Death', a plague against which victims had very little resistance. It was spread by fleas hosted by black rats and probably originated in the spring of 1346 in the steppe region of Eastern Europe. From there it was transmitted along trade routes to European ports and on by ship to most European countries. After a three-day incubation period, a victim felt ill and developed painful boils (buboes) in the groin, armpit, thigh or neck, and after three to five days, 80% of the victims would die. The disease reached Bordeaux by March 1348 and a ship from there arrived at Melcombe Regis, near Weymouth, in May and the plague probably broke out from there in June and reached London in August. Its severity was unprecedented and the death toll was so high and so unexpected that it tended to be viewed fatalistically by many as a divine judgement.[7]

It is not unlikely that in this first visitation of the plague in England, lasting from the summer of 1348 to that of 1349, at least 30% of the population of around 4.5 million died. In other countries of Europe, the percentage of those who died was probably much the same. Though this initial outbreak of the plague was the severest, the disease recurred regularly in Europe until the eighteenth century, with the worst outbreaks in the Montagu period being from 1360 to 1363 and in 1374 and 1400.[8]

The plague did not spare Edward III's family because his daughter, Joan, who was on her way by ship to marry the heir to the crown of Castile, as the result of negotiations begun in 1343 by the first Earl of Salisbury, died of the plague in Bordeaux on 1 July and Edward's infant son William died at Windsor soon afterwards. Edward's court stayed away from London and spent much of the time at royal manors in the country but the king made sure that the first formal meeting of his new Garter knights took place in 1349 at Windsor on 23 April, St George's Day, where the Earl of Salisbury, resplendent in armour, blue cloak and red turbaned hat, played his due part in the religious solemnities and festive celebrations.

In July 1349, shortly after his twenty-first birthday, Salisbury was confirmed in his inheritance and ceased to be a ward of the king, which meant that he became fully responsible for the properties inherited from his father. Shortly after this, however, came bad news from

The second Earl of Salisbury, one of the founding members of the Order of the Garter, from the Bruges Garter Book, c.1430

Avignon, where Pope Clement VI had annulled Salisbury's marriage to Joan of Kent and recognized her earlier marriage to Sir Thomas Holland. So Joan left Salisbury and lived with Holland until his death in 1360, bearing him four surviving children, two boys and two girls. Salisbury wasted no time in finding a second wife and soon married Elizabeth, the daughter of John de Mohun, lord of Dunster, who was about fifteen at the time. It proved to be a happy and lasting union, producing a son, yet another William, and two daughters.

In August 1350 Philip VI of France died, to be succeeded by his thirty-one-year-old son John II, whose wife had just died from the plague. Edward was dissuaded by his advisers from renewing the war on French soil but took advantage instead of a perceived threat from Castile, under its new king, Peter I, who had become an ally of the French. Edward assembled a fleet of about 50 cogs which he kept at sea near Sandwich and used to attack a Castilian fleet laden with Flemish goods on 29 August off Winchelsea. Using grappling tactics against the larger Spanish ships the English men-at-arms won a decisive victory and several Spanish vessels were captured. Salisbury provided a military contingent for this battle and himself commanded one of the ships, but his relative youth and inexperience meant that he played a subordinate role to the king and his seasoned commanders, the earls of Lancaster, Northampton and Warwick.[9]

The loss of several Montagu estates

After the naval victory at Winchelsea, Edward III did not go to war for another six years, concentrating instead on the many problems caused at home by the Black Death and its economic implications. The fact that there were fewer men available to work for their lords in accordance with feudal obligations led to a gradual change in the social system, as labourers became more aware of their value and ability to demand cash payment for their work. Unrest and lawlessness in the countryside, a problem that Edward III had inherited from his father's turbulent reign, was gradually addressed by granting local squires extensive powers as 'justices of the peace'. A third problem, the unpopular high taxes which Edward had imposed to fund his wars, was tackled by recruiting able ministers to replenish the royal revenues.

During this relatively peaceful period it is likely that the Earl of Salisbury concentrated his attentions on his new wife and growing family and also addressed the vital question of his inheritance. Between the time of his father's death in 1344 and his own coming of age in 1349 the extensive Montagu lands had been under the direct control of the king, whose agents, headed by Salisbury's appointed guardian, Sir John Wingfield, would have been fully responsible for their administration.[10] The wardship of a minor could be a dangerous time for a landed family because some lords who were granted wardships could be unscrupulous, diverting revenues from the ward's lands to their own coffers. Even kings could not necessarily be trusted in this respect, especially if they were short of money. Moreover, the effective administration of extensive landholdings depended a great deal on the energy and ability of the lord who owned them and in 1350 Salisbury was still only 22 and relatively inexperienced. One interesting issue is whether the Isle of Man came under the wardship of the king between 1344 and 1349 or whether, because of its special status, it remained outside royal jurisdiction. The fact that there seem to be no documents relevant to it in the royal archives for this period perhaps suggests the latter.

Salisbury must have been aware that his father had been 'crowned' king of the Manx and a young man of any mettle would surely have visited the Island as soon as possible to establish his position there. The third Earl of Moray had been killed at Neville's Cross without leaving an heir, so there was no theoretical rival to the Salisbury claim to the Island. Also, since the capture of David II at that battle, the threat of any Scottish interference in the Island had very much receded. Hence it would seem likely that Salisbury would have visited the Isle of Man at some time between 1350 and 1356 to lay claim to his 'kingdom' and possibly be crowned there as well as receiving the homage of his chief tenants, inspecting his two castles and perhaps meeting the bishop and the abbot of Rushen.

One of the major issues concerning Salisbury's inherited estates was that several of them had been the property of men who had fallen from grace in the early part of Edward's reign but who recovered royal favour after 1344. As early as 1346 the king decided to return Salisbury's manor of Stoke Trister in Somerset, which he had granted to the first earl, to Sir John Molyns, a supporter of archbishop Stratford in 1341 whom the first earl had arrested on the king's authority. Five years later, this clearly seemed an injustice to the king.[11]

A far more serious problem for Salisbury arose over his rights to the lordship of Denbigh. After Edward I's conquest of North Wales, the king granted the cantreds of Ros and Reywynnock to Henry de Lacy, Earl of Lincoln, and it was he who employed the military architect James of St George to construct a formidable and extensive castle on the hilltop overlooking the small town of Denbigh from 1282 onwards. Within fifty years the lordship and castle changed hands four times, reflecting the turbulent politics of the age. Lincoln left no son and his heiress, Alice, married Thomas, Earl of Lancaster. After his execution and the forfeiture of his lands, the Denbigh lordship was granted to Hugh Despenser the elder, Earl of Winchester, and after his execution in 1326 it was granted to Roger Mortimer, the first Earl of March. On his fall and execution in 1330 a grateful Edward III granted it to Salisbury's father, as we have seen. By this time the lordship extended over a good deal of north-east Wales and included the smaller castles of Mold and Hawarden.

In the parliament of 1352 Edward III agreed to issue a Statute of Treasons which more narrowly defined treason in the face of anxieties among the nobility that, as had been shown many times in the past, great lords and their estates could fall victim to the whim of a ruthless monarch. Roger Mortimer, the namesake and grandson of Isabella's lover, was born in the same year as Salisbury, fought at Crécy in 1346 and became, despite his youth, a confidant of the king, who appointed him a founder member of the Order of the Garter. When, early in 1350, Edward III took a small party with him to Calais on a potentially dangerous mission to thwart a plot to betray the town, Roger Mortimer was by his side and after 1352 Mortimer began to press for the cancellation of the attainder against his grandfather's titles and lands, arguing that he had been summarily executed without a fair trial.

In 1354 parliament overturned the attainder and Mortimer succeeded to the title of Earl of March. He then began to seek restitution of as much of the former Mortimer lands as he could get his hands on. In this quest he was supported by the king and Salisbury's legal arguments and objections were eventually dismissed, so that the lordship of Denbigh was restored to Mortimer, without compensation. What lay behind Edward's thinking here is difficult to determine. It was not necessarily a personal matter of his favouring Mortimer more than Salisbury but more probably a calculated political decision to avoid the re-opening of ancient animosities.[12]

The loss of Denbigh was soon followed by a contest over another valuable Montagu property, the town and castle of Sherborne, in Dorset. This had been granted by the king to William Montagu in 1330 as a reward for his support but in 1355 the bishop of Salisbury, Robert Wyvill, argued in the Court of Common Pleas that it belonged historically to the bishops of Salisbury, who had never renounced their right to it. The earl's colourful response was to offer to settle the matter by single combat between the claimants' champions, and to this purpose, both the bishop and the Earl of Salisbury, accompanied by their champions, met at the appointed place and time. On inspection of the bishop's champion, he was found to have had 'several rolls of prayer and charms' about his person so the combat was postponed until the following day when the earl's champion failed to show up and judgement was passed against the earl by default. It seems that a deal had been done 'out of court' because the bishop subsequently paid 2,500 marks for the release of the earl's rights in Sherborne. The bishop's funeral brass in Salisbury Cathedral can still be seen today showing him triumphantly ensconced in his castle.[13]

Poitiers and Brétigny, 1356-1360

During the years 1351 and 1352 great gains were made both in Aquitaine and Brittany by English forces and their allies under Sir Walter Bentley and the Earl of Stafford, who won a notable victory over the French and Bretons at Mauron in August 1352. Anglo-French negotiations produced peace proposals at Guines in 1354 and Avignon in 1355 but Edward instead decided to re-open the war by supporting Charles, King of Navarre, who appealed to him for support in his personal rivalry with John II of France. For his part, John II was also keen to re-open hostilities to avenge the humiliation of Crécy. In the autumn of 1355 Edward III equipped an expedition headed by the Prince of Wales, whom he appointed as regent of Aquitaine. Popular history knows him as 'The 'Black Prince', but this seems to have been a name given to him by the antiquarian John Leland nearly two hundred years later and for reasons that are obscure. It was certainly not a name used during his lifetime. Prince Edward was now twenty-five and already a seasoned warrior admired for his magnificent presence, his prowess as a fighter and his chivalric reputation.[14]

The Earl of Salisbury, along with Thomas de Beauchamp, the Earl of Warwick, went with the prince as his chief commanders and they arrived at Bordeaux on 20 September. Soon afterwards the prince's Anglo-Gascon army set out on a plundering raid, or 'chevauchée', in three divisions, with Warwick leading, the prince in the centre and Salisbury in the rear. Devastating the towns and countryside as they went, they reached Carcassonne and also recruited the support of the Count of Foix. Sir John Wingfield, the former guardian of Salisbury who was now part of the prince's retinue, wrote to the Bishop of Winchester on 23 December: 'It seems certain that since the war against the French king began, there has never been such destruction in a region as in this raid. For the countryside and towns which have been destroyed in this raid produced more revenue for the king of France in aid of his wars than half his kingdom...'[15]

This war strategy of the 'chevauchée', a series of continuing raids with the main aim being devastation masquerading as deeds of chivalric glory, is described with relish by the herald of Sir John Chandos, one of Prince Edward's closest friends and companions-in-arms, who wrote of this campaign that having arrived in Bordeaux, the prince:

> was soon ready to put an army of six thousand men in the field. He rode towards Toulouse: there were no towns which he did not lay waste. He took Carcassonne, Béziers and Narbonne and laid waste and harried all the countryside as well as many towns and castles, which did not please his enemies in Gascony. He was in the field for four and a half months or more and did great damage....Then the prince returned to Bordeaux and stayed there until the winter was past. He and his noble knights lived in great happiness and joy. There were gay, noble, courteous, good and generous men there: and he put his men in winter quarters in the castles nearby. Warwick was at La Reole, Salisbury at Ste Foy, Suffolk at St Emilion, and his men were lodged at Libourne and all around.[16]

In June 1356 Henry, Duke of Lancaster, crossed to Normandy with another English army and won several minor successes against enemy strongholds, while in August Prince Edward set out from the south to join forces with him. John II ordered the bridges across the Loire to be destroyed, which prevented Lancaster from marching south, and on 18 September King John confronted the English outside the town of Poitiers. Again, the prince divided his army of between six and eight thousand men into three divisions: the van was led by the earls of Warwick and Oxford and the Gascon Captal de Buch, the centre by the prince and the rear by the earls of Suffolk and Salisbury. The French army, which was considerably larger than the English, was led by John II, his young heir the dauphin, the Duke of Orléans and the marshals Audrehem and Clermont.[17] When the Earl of Warwick in the van appeared to retreat, in fact to guard the army's baggage train, the French again made the mistake of launching a hasty series of cavalry charges, one of them against Salisbury's division. The herald of Sir John Chandos has left us this contemporary account of the part played by Salisbury in the battle:

> Then the clamour and the shouting began and the two armies approached each other. On both sides swords were drawn and lances couched: no-one did not join in. The Earl of Salisbury, so I am told, led the prince's rearguard; but that day he was the first to join battle because the marshals, full of anger and bad temper, attacked him on foot and on horseback. When the earl saw their troops he turned his battalion towards them and cried 'Advance, my lords, in God's name, since St George wills that although we were the last, we should be the first to fight; and let us do deeds that will win us honour'. So the barons hurled themselves into the battle; if you had no part in the battle, it would have been a fine thing to watch, but it was a sad and harsh sight as well....The book and the story tell how the Earl of Salisbury and his companions, who fought more fiercely than lions, defeated the marshals and the armed cavalry before the vanguard could wheel round and come back over the river which they had just crossed. But they all

The second Earl of Salisbury, linked by a silver chain (see page 40) to his wife, Elizabeth (née Mohun), who is standing on what may be a depiction of the Isle of Man. Her husband quartered the three legs of Man on his arms, displayed here on his surcoat.

assembled together and came on in a noble band up the hill until their ranks were facing the dauphin's battalion, which was going through a gap in a little hedge. They came on steadily and did such deeds of arms that it was wonderful to watch. They captured the gap in the hedge by their attack, which dismayed the French, who began to turn their backs and mount their horses. There were shouts everywhere of 'Guyenne! St George!' The Normandy battalion was defeated while it was still morning and the dauphin left the field. [18]

Hence Salisbury foiled the initial French charge and all of the subsequent French advances proved unsuccessful. John II's decision to send his men-at-arms into action at this point proved to be another serious mistake and after prolonged hand-to-hand fighting he was forced to surrender and taken into the custody of the Earl of Warwick. In addition, John's younger son Philip was captured, along with eight counts, one archbishop and the French marshal, Audrehem. Prince Edward cemented his reputation as the flower of European chivalry by treating his prisoners with elaborate courtesy and proclaiming John II as the hero of the contest. Geoffrey le Baker was impressed with Salisbury's performance. 'Those lions, the earls of Warwick and Salisbury' he wrote, 'competed to see which of them could flood the soil of Poitou with more draughts of French blood, and which of them could boast that his weapons were more deeply stained with the warm blood of Frenchmen.'[19]

The result of Poitiers meant that Edward III now held captive the kings of the two nations against whom he had waged war for the greater part of his reign. In May 1357 Prince Edward entered London with John II, where he was greeted with a display of pomp and magnificence by the citizens. At a lavish banquet subsequently held in Westminster, Edward III sat between his two prisoners, the King of France on his right and the King of Scotland on his left and both were the chief guests at an elaborate tournament held at Smithfield in October. Although both prisoners were treated with great honour and dignity, much of the diplomacy of the next few months was centred on the matter of their ransoms, for which Edward was personally responsible. The ransoms of all the other captives taken in Scotland and in France were mostly a matter for settlement between captor and captives. We do not know whether the Earl of Salisbury was lucky enough to take illustrious prisoners at Poitiers and to benefit financially from their ransoms, but it is at least possible that he did. The Earl of Warwick, for instance, who had initially taken custody of John II, profited greatly and spent a good deal of the money on magnificent fortifications at Warwick Castle, most of which can still be seen today.

The ransom of David II was settled by the Treaty of Berwick in October 1357 by which it was agreed that he would be released for a payment of 100,000 marks, or £66,667, to be paid in instalments over ten years and guaranteed by hostages. Moreover, the settlement emphasised the rights of a number of Edward III's loyal supporters to Scottish properties such as the estates of the former disinherited lords. The treaty also included a vigorous defence of the Earl of Salisbury's claim to the Isle of Man.[20] In January 1358 negotiators suggested a ransom of a million marks, (or £666,667, or four million écus) for John II but his son the Dauphin Charles had to deal not only with rebellious nobles but also in May and June of 1358 the 'Jacquerie', a savage and unexpected rising of thousands of peasants in northern France who brutally murdered members of the nobility and gentry wherever they could find them. Negotiations stalled and Edward III decided in 1359 to make use of the weakness of the dauphin's rule to invade France again. The army he raised was full of illustrious names, including his four eldest sons, his cousin Henry of Lancaster, five earls, including Salisbury and the Earl of March, who held the title of marshal of the army, and many other lords and knights.

Edward crossed with this force to Calais late in October and made for Rheims but found that it was too well defended to capture. In January 1360 the king marched south to Burgundy where the Earl of March, aged 31, died suddenly of disease. Two months later the English returned to Paris in an attempt to confront the dauphin and bring him to battle, but Charles refused to fight and Edward withdrew to Chartres where his army was weakened and demoralised by bad weather and disease. In May, at the small village of Brétigny, a peace treaty was agreed by which Edward would give up his claim to the French throne in return for sovereign rights over Aquitaine, Poitou, Ponthieu and Calais, as well as lesser provinces and payment of a ransom of £500,000 for John II. In July Edward appointed negotiators to meet the French at Calais and work out the details of the agreement and these included Prince Edward, Prince Lionel, the Duke of Lancaster and the earls of Arundel, Stafford and Salisbury. Edward III and John II arrived later to set their seals on the resulting 'Treaty of Calais' and there was much feasting and magnificent entertainment. Edward had won sovereign rule over about a third of France, which was a great achievement, but his renunciation of the French throne was seen as a sell-out by some of his supporters, especially on the continent.

As for the second Earl of Salisbury, he had surely made a success of his life, so far. He had fought at Crécy and taken part in the siege of Calais and the naval victory at Winchelsea. He had enjoyed the great honour of being one of the founding members of the Order of the Garter and he had been one of Prince Edward's chief commanders in the successful chevauchées of 1355 in southern France. His role in the battle of Poitiers had shown him to be a capable leader of the army's rear division and a brave and determined warrior. Subsequently he was entrusted by the king with the important task of being one of the main negotiators at the Treaty of Calais. Regarding his own inheritance, he had successfully established control over most of his inherited estates as well as the lordship of Man, but had lost the lordships of Denbigh, Sherborne and some lesser manors, largely because he did not have the implicit support of the king in these disputed cases. Finally, he had dramatically lost his first wife, Joan of Kent, to Sir Thomas Holland in a process that must have caused him considerable personal distress. So he had not had an easy life, but at the age of 32 and despite a number of major disappointments, he was still one of the king's most loyal supporters as a warrior and negotiator, and a leading figure in English national life.

Years of peace, 1360-1369

King John returned to France in 1360 leaving his son Louis of Anjou as a hostage for the payment of his ransom. But Louis escaped in 1363 and John, conscious of the dishonour of this action and also the fact that very little of his ransom had as yet been paid, took the remarkable decision to return voluntarily to England as a prisoner in 1364. Once in London, however, he contracted an illness of which he died in April that year. His body was returned to France where his able and energetic son, the former dauphin, succeeded him as Charles V. With the help of the formidable military expert Bertrand du Guesclin he began the process of rebuilding a nation shattered by catastrophic military defeats, a king in prison, rebellious lords, the 'Jacquerie' and the plague.

In 1361 the Prince of Wales shocked the contemporary world, and especially his parents, by announcing his intention to marry Joan of Kent. She had, of course, been married to Salisbury between 1341 and 1349 and then the much older Thomas Holland, who died in 1360. She was by now 33 and the prince was 31 and the marriage was regarded by many as unsuitable, if not scandalous. However, they had been brought up together and the prince had always admired her. Salisbury and his wife no doubt attended the splendid marriage ceremony at Windsor, perhaps with mixed feelings, and in the following year the king created his son Prince of Aquitaine, a new title which, in defiance of Charles V, implied that the new prince was the 'ruler of an independent territory held under the direct lordship of the crown of England'.[21] He and Joan presided over a brilliant court at Bordeaux, famous for its extravagance and devotion to chivalry, but the prince proved to be an unwise administrator. He caused grave offence to the local lords by increasing taxation and imposing unwelcome reforms in his attempt to set up a centralized government – something that ran counter to local traditions.

The prince eventually escaped from the tedium of administration by supporting his father's ally Peter I of Castile, who was deposed by his half-brother and rival Henry of Trastámara, with French support. Doing what he did best, in April 1367 the prince won the great victory of Nájera in the Castilian province of La Rioja, again largely because the French part of Trastámara's army made disorganized and premature cavalry charges that suffered disastrous losses. Many captives were taken, though Trastámara escaped. Peter was restored as king of Castile but Prince Edward was not impressed by his treachery, brutality and failure to pay for the costs of the Nájera campaign. Trastámara returned to Castile in 1368 and succeeded in besieging Peter in the fortress of Montiel. He then lured Peter to his tent, ostensibly to negotiate, and there stabbed him to death, which some thought a not unsuitable end for a ruler known in Spain as 'Pedro el Cruel'.

A good deal of Prince Edward's army was composed of English mercenary forces and there is no reason why, had he wanted to do so, the Earl of Salisbury could not have taken a detachment of his own men

A romantic nineteenth-century engraving of St Patrick's Isle at Peel, on the Isle of Man. The fortifications enclose the medieval cathedral and were strengthened by the second Earl of Salisbury in the 1360s. Painted by William Leighton Leitch and engraved by William Miller, 1845.

to fight in Aquitaine or Spain. But he chose not to pursue a military career during this decade and devoted himself to domestic responsibilities and to fulfilling his obligations as a great landowner. In 1361 he served as a justice of the peace in Hampshire and Somerset and in 1362 and 1364 he was a JP in Dorset. In 1367 he served on a commission of array in Somerset and another commission tasked with scrutinizing the border between the counties of Somerset and Devon: in 1368 he was again a JP in Dorset.[22] In these roles as a JP he was exercising comparatively new powers given to local landowners by the king in an attempt to tackle a problem that had bedevilled the nation since the beginning of the century – widespread lawlessness caused by bands of brigands and marauders who roamed the countryside at will.

The Irish Sea was also under constant threat from pirates and adventurers from Ireland, Scotland and even France and in 1363 the Manx bishop, William Russell, wrote an official complaint to the Pope that the cathedral precincts on St Patrick's Isle in Peel had been 'seriously disturbed' by the building of military fortifications. Russell, who may have been Manx, became abbot of Rushen in 1330 and was consecrated bishop of Sodor and Man by Clement VI in Avignon in 1349. As abbot of Rushen and then bishop from 1330 to his death in 1374 he was a major figure in the ecclesiastical governance of the Island under the first two earls of Salisbury. His complaint now had arisen because the second earl had initiated a programme of defensive works at Peel which the bishop felt was not entirely in the interests of the diocese. Just how extensive these works were is difficult to determine exactly, but the most recent overview of the Island's archaeology is of the opinion that a good many of the defensive buildings at Peel were probably constructed during the lordship of the second Earl of Salisbury. These include the strengthening of the outer walls, the construction of several tower houses and possibly the crenellation of the cathedral itself.[23]

To placate the Pope and the bishop Salisbury co-operated with the Irish provincial prior of the Franciscans and in 1367 petitioned the Pope for permission to build for the Dublin order of Friars Minor:

> A church or oratory, together with a bell-tower, bell, cemetery, houses and other necessary offices, provided that twelve brethren of the said order can be fittingly and

properly maintained at the place, without however infringing on the rights of the parochial church.[24]

The Pope gave his consent and Salisbury provided a site at Bemaken, near Ballabeg, where the priory was completed by 1373, together with about 40 acres of land for which the monks paid twenty shillings annual rent to the Lord of Man.[25]

But Salisbury's main building work on the Island was undertaken at Castle Rushen. An architectural and archaeological survey completed in 2012 for Manx National Heritage has concluded that the original structure was a square stone tower, built probably by King Reginald I of Man, who died in 1228. The Dublin Chronicle stated that the tower was destroyed by Robert Bruce in 1313, but this seems to have been an exaggeration, because the lower portions of the present keep contain much stone from the thirteenth century. The first earl probably inherited a considerable 'stump' which had been badly damaged and suffered from neglect. Work on its repair may have begun in his lifetime, but it certainly proceeded under his son. First of all the existing stump was raised considerably in height and towers were added on the south and west sides. Then the ground within the tower was raised to its present level and a new entrance gateway was built. Soon after this the keep was increased in height to the present three storeys and a further tower built on the east side, with an additional north gatehouse.

From the 1360s to the 1380s the existing curtain wall was built, supported by towers with firing platforms and gun ports, and the present outer gatehouse and barbican were constructed, with a ditch beyond the curtain wall. The work was probably done in stages and the cost would have been borne by the earl, so it is surely likely that he would have taken a personal interest and made visits to the Island to see how it was progressing. As a soldier with a great deal of experience of siege warfare he would have been well placed to supervise the rebuilding programme.[26]

During the early 1360s Salisbury was involved in yet another complicated legal dispute concerning his English estates. In 1337 Edward III had granted his father the reversion to a clutch of valuable West Country properties which included the castle and manor of Trowbridge, the manors of Aldbourne, Amesbury and Winterborne in Wiltshire, Canford in Dorset and Henstridge and Charlton in Somerset. These

An early twentieth-century image of Castle Rushen in Castletown on the Isle of Man. Recent research has concluded that the first castle on this site was a square stone keep, probably built in the reign of Reginald I, King of Man (1187-1228). The Montagus inherited this structure, perhaps in a damaged or neglected state, and gradually increased its size and strength with the addition of the towers, barbican and curtain walls that can be seen in this picture.

manors had been held by Thomas of Lancaster but after his execution and attainder they had been granted to the Warenne family, with a reversion to the Montagus. The manors in fact reverted to Salisbury in 1361 but in that year Henry, Duke of Lancaster, died without leaving a male heir and his vast estates and title passed to the king's fourth son John of Gaunt, who had married Lancaster's heiress, Blanche, two years previously. In 1365 Gaunt claimed in the Court of King's Bench that the estates in question had belonged to his wife's grandfather, Thomas of Lancaster, and that on the same principle the estates of Roger Mortimer had been restored to the second Earl of March, these estates should be restored to him as Duke of Lancaster. In July 1365 the court gave judgement in Gaunt's favour and it seems that the two litigants agreed a compromise by which Lancaster took Trowbridge and Aldbourne for himself and allowed Salisbury to hold the rest of the estates as his tenant. Even so, this was another serious loss of property for Salisbury.[27]

War again, 1369-1382

Salisbury's main involvement on the international stage during the 1360s was the part he played as a negotiator in the important discussions which began in 1364, aimed at securing a marriage alliance between Edward III's son Edmund of Langley and Margaret of Flanders, the ten-year-old heiress to Flanders, Brabant, Artois and Burgundy.[28] If achieved, this would have created a powerful Anglo-Flemish satellite state as a counter-balance to the French and Salisbury served on deputations under the bishop of London and John of Gaunt which led to the Treaty of Dover, setting up the alliance. However, the pro-French papacy at Avignon refused to licence a marriage which was so clearly not in the interests of John II of France, who sought a marriage between Margaret and his son Philip. As a result of papal procrastination the Anglo-Flemish marriage was delayed and had eventually to be abandoned. Margaret did marry Philip, while Edmund married Isabella of Castile.[29] This affair caused serious hostility between England and France and Edward III on more than one occasion threatened to go to war over the issue.

It is clear that Salisbury was one of the king's closest advisers at this time because at Christmas 1368 he was with the king and members of the royal family at Windsor, together with the chancellor, William of

Wykeham (bishop of Winchester), the treasurer, John Barnet (bishop of Ely), and the earls of Warwick, Oxford and Arundel. Together with them he remained with the king in the New Year when the court moved first to Sheen and then to Westminster. Though Edward was suffering from illness at this time and also mourning the recent death of his son Lionel, he spent much of this period discussing the options for future hostilities with France with these trusted confidants.[30]

In the end it was unrest in Aquitaine which resulted in the renewal of war. In 1369 Prince Edward's reforming policies led to a revolt against him of several of the barons there, who appealed to Charles V of France as their overlord, despite the terms of the Treaty of Brétigny. Ignoring the treaty, Charles summoned Edward to hear their case and when he refused the prince was denounced as a 'contumacious vassal' and his rights to Aquitaine were declared forfeit. This led Edward III, with the full support of the English parliament, to resume his title to the French throne and prepare again for war. But by now the king had lost most of his earlier energy and skill and become increasingly lethargic. His wife died in this year and for his last seven years he fell under the influence of his highly unpopular young mistress, Alice Perrers, whose main interest in life was the accumulation of influence and properties for herself.

Given that Salisbury had recently been locked in a legal dispute with the Duke of Lancaster, it was a sign of his unswerving loyalty to the crown that he responded to the call to arms which resulted in his being one of the commanders of the army of about 6,000 men headed by Lancaster which assembled in Calais in September 1369. Lancaster was unable to force the French to fight and instead resorted to 'chevauchée' tactics that destroyed much of the Norman countryside but otherwise achieved very little, at great expense. In 1370 Prince Edward, from his base in Aquitaine, attacked Limoges which he subjected to a degree of destruction and brutality that did nothing to win the sympathy of the French and eroded his reputation for chivalrous dealing. He had fallen ill with a persistent form of dysentery in Spain during the Najerá campaign, and still a sick man he now returned to England and never went on campaign again. With both the king and his heir deprived of their former fighting abilities, the English were on the back foot, especially given the resurgence in French military power engineered by Charles V and Bertrand du Guesclin, who made good use of the lessons in military tactics learned at Crécy and Poitiers. Moreover, with Prince Edward gone from Aquitaine many lords switched their allegiance to Charles V and by 1372 only a strip of the coastline between Bordeaux and Bayonne remained under English control.

The Duke of Lancaster's first wife, Blanche, died in 1368 at the age of 23 and in 1371 he married Constanza, the elder daughter and heiress of the murdered Peter I of Castile. As a result Edward III and the English parliament recognized his claim to the title of King of Castile, even though the pro-French Henry of Trastámara was firmly in power there. Hence English war aims became divided between Edward III's attempt to be recognized as King of France, Prince Edward's claim to be the ruler of Aquitaine and the Duke of Lancaster's claim in Castile. In 1372 the threat emerged of a Franco-Spanish naval invasion of English shores and in April the Earl of Salisbury sealed an indenture to serve for a full year and provide 120 men-at-arms and 200 archers, evidence that he was certainly a great and wealthy lord at this time.[31] Meanwhile, the Spanish threat was shown to be a reality when in June a small fleet under the Earl of Pembroke was destroyed by the Spanish off La Rochelle, and Pembroke was imprisoned under ignominious conditions by Henry of Trastámara.

Edward III's hostility to Trastámara was further illustrated by the marriage of his son Edmund to Peter I's younger daughter, Isabella, at Wallingford Castle in July, where probably Salisbury was an honoured guest. In August 1372 Salisbury was called to support a force which was intended to be led by the king in person and he sailed with his contingent from Poole and mustered at Sandwich with the rest of the expedition, but exceptionally bad weather forced its cancellation in October, much to the chagrin of the king. In February 1373 Salisbury achieved some notable successes after being appointed commander of a fleet tasked with guarding the Channel. Sailing from Cornwall he surprised and burned seven Castilian ships in St Malo and then sailed on to Brest, which was being besieged by du Guesclin. There he was able to bring supplies and reinforcements to the town before returning to his task of patrolling the Channel.[32]

With the king and Prince Edward ailing men, John of Gaunt took up the role of chief royal warrior and led another army across the Channel in July 1373, which failed to make any impact in northern France, and then rode on a grand 'chevauchée' down to Aquitaine, where he was unable to restore English control. Lancaster might have contemplated crossing the Pyrenees in 1374 to advance his claims to the kingdom of Castile but his father was not prepared to finance these ambitions and he returned to England. By now it was clear that most of the English gains made in France during Edward III's reign had been lost, the house of Valois was again in the ascendant, the ageing English king was surrounded by an unpopular clique of courtiers and there was widespread resentment across England at the endless demands for taxes to finance what now seemed to be fruitless wars.

Pope Gregory XI, elected in 1370, had constantly sought peace between England and France and during 1374 negotiations took place under the sponsorship of papal envoys, leading to a conference in Bruges in March 1375, which suggested terms which Edward III found unacceptable. Salisbury played a significant part in these discussions and together with a very prestigious deputation consisting of Lancaster, the archbishop of Canterbury, the Earl of Cambridge and lords Latimer and Cobham, he went a second time to Bruges on the king's orders to negotiate a more acceptable settlement. Detailed proposals were debated for three months but in the end the only agreement reached was a truce until the beginning of April 1377.[33]

Public criticism of the royal administration, which had simmered for years, was voiced in the so-called 'Good Parliament' which met for a record ten weeks in the early summer of 1376. The king's request for money was debated by the Commons in the chapter house of Westminster Abbey, where they refused to vote new taxes and elected (for the first time) a Speaker, Sir Peter de la Mare, who would convey this unwelcome news to the king. The Commons went on to 'impeach' a number of the king's most unpopular advisers, which ultimately resulted in the dismissal of lords Latimer and Neville, the imprisonment of Sir Richard Lyons and the banishment from the court of Alice Perrers. The public mood had been made clear and important precedents had been set, but the parliament called in January 1377, faced with the hostility of the Duke of Lancaster, was far less critical, pardoned the offenders and agreed to the imposition of a 'poll' tax of four pence on all lay persons over the age of fourteen. Along with the earls of Arundel, Warwick and Stafford, as well as other lords, Salisbury was chosen by the government to impress upon the Commons the need for restraint and co-operation, especially faced with the prospect of renewed war with France.³⁴ He also served as a commissioner of array and peace in Dorset early in the year and attended a meeting of the great council in April.³⁵

At the age of 45, Prince Edward had died on 8 June 1376 from the results of the illness that had afflicted him for nearly ten years and his father followed him on 21 June 1377, aged 64. Edward III reigned for fifty years and after a shaky start won military successes that made him the most respected ruler of his day and an English monarchical paragon until revisionist historians of the Victorian period argued that he was far too fond of self-aggrandisement at the expense of the welfare of his people. Modern scholars tend to take the view that in his prime he was a very great ruler in terms of personal leadership, both military and political, but that his later years were a major disappointment. The first Earl of Salisbury was his chief mentor and friend up to 1344, while the second earl, only a boy at his father's death, steadily won the king's high regard through distinguished and unfalteringly loyal service as a warrior and diplomat, despite the fact that he often received less than generous support from the king over his disputed marriage and contested inheritance.

A new reign, 1377

The Earl of Salisbury had a very unusual connection with the new king because he was the son of Joan of Kent, who had once been William's wife. After her marriage to the Prince of Wales in 1361 she went out with her husband to govern Aquitaine and in Angoulême their first child was born, a son called Edward, who lived only from 1365 to 1370. His younger brother, Richard, was born in January 1367 in Bordeaux (when Joan was 38) and it was he who now succeeded at the age of ten to his grandfather's throne as Richard II.

In the absence of hard and fast rules about the minority of English kings, the natural choice as Richard's guardian, or even as regent, might have been his uncle John of Gaunt, Duke of Lancaster, who had effectively governed the country during the last months of his father's illness. Edward's two elder sons were dead – Lionel, Duke of Clarence in 1368 and the Prince of Wales in 1376, which left Lancaster, Edmund, Earl of Cambridge, and Thomas, Earl of Buckingham as the new king's three surviving uncles. Lancaster's great power and influence was viewed with suspicion by some of the nobility as well as members of the higher clergy and the citizens of London, who had sacked his home, the Savoy Palace, in protest against reprisals he had taken against members of the 'Good Parliament' and also his support for the heretical teachings of those early 'Protestants', known as the Lollards.

Aware of his unpopularity and its dangers, Lancaster made peace with his critics and accepted the general view that government should be carried on in the young king's name by a series of 'continuing councils' composed of a small number of lords, bishops and knights. In July 1377 the boy king was crowned in a magnificent ceremony in Westminster Abbey which emphasised his right to succeed by birth and anointed him as the divinely appointed guardian of the realm. Salisbury, with the other earls, and robed in white as a symbol of innocence and childlike purity, took part in an elaborate and impressive procession through London beforehand and paid homage to the new king after his crowning.[36] On the same day as his coronation, the king created five new earls, one of whom was his half-brother Thomas Holland, who became Earl of Kent.

The truce with France had come to an end only three days after the start of the new reign and the French had long been preparing for the renewal of the conflict with a three-pronged assault. At the beginning of July many English Channel ports were attacked by a French fleet and both Calais and Bordeaux were besieged, though they did not capitulate. Immediately after the coronation the government sent reinforcements to the Channel ports, including two hundred men-at-arms and three hundred archers who were sent to Pevensey under the command of the Earl of Salisbury and his brother Sir John Montagu.[37] In January 1378 the government equipped a major force under the command of Lancaster, Salisbury and Arundel but it did not set sail for three months because Lancaster was occupied with the charms of his mistress, Catherine Swynford, so his critics claimed. Salisbury and Arundel eventually set out without him in April and sailed to Harfleur, where they were repulsed by the locals, and then on to Cherbourg where they failed to capture a Spanish vessel. Lancaster joined them in July, when they attacked the Norman coast and St Malo, but without success.

Also in 1378 Charles, King of Navarre, sought an alliance with England to protect him against the French but in return the government demanded the port of Cherbourg, in Normandy, held by the Navarrese, and Salisbury contracted to provide men to garrison the town, which took place in the summer. This meant that although the English had largely been expelled from the hinterland of France, they still had important toe-holds at Calais, Brest, Cherbourg, Bordeaux and Bayonne, all of which were expensive to maintain but strategically vital. From 1379 to 1380 Salisbury was appointed to the important post of Captain of Calais and sent troops to capture and burn the fortified French monastery at Beaulieu. On his return to England in 1380 he again returned to his duties as commissioner of array and peace in Dorset and in Wiltshire the following year.[38]

Being a commissioner for peace in the counties suddenly became a very dangerous business early in June 1381 when agricultural workers and artisans from Essex and Kent rose in protest at the imposition of a poll tax of one shilling per adult and soon chose as their leaders Wat Tyler, an able man and possibly a former soldier, and John Ball, an eloquent but fanatical priest. The protesters marched on London and were on the outskirts by 12 June, demanding to see the king. Accompanied by Salisbury, Warwick, Oxford and other advisers, the fourteen-year-old king was rowed in his royal barge to Rotherhithe but found the rebels to be in their thousands, hostile and loud in their demands for the heads of Lancaster (who was in Berwick at the time) and other unpopular ministers. According to Froissart:

> When the king and his nobles saw the frenzied crowds on the bank, the boldest of them were frightened and his barons advised the king not to land. They began to turn the barge away and upstream again. The king called 'Sirs, what have you to say to me? Tell me. I came here to talk to you.' Those who could hear him shouted with one voice: 'Come on land, you! It will be easier that way to tell you what we want'. The Earl of Salisbury, speaking for the king, replied: 'Sirs, you are not in a fit condition for the king to talk to you now'. Nothing was added to this and the king went back, as advised, to the Tower of London, from where he had started. [39]

The departure of the royal barge prompted the mob to march on London the same day, sack the Marshalsea prison and the archbishop's palace at Lambeth and then cross London Bridge into the heart of the city, where they released inmates of the Fleet prison, pillaged the lawyers' chambers in the Temple and then attacked the Duke of Lancaster's Savoy Palace and burnt it to the ground. The king, safe for the time being in the Tower of London, climbed to its upper ramparts and watched the chaos with the Earl of Salisbury and other counsellors. Sir William Walworth, the Lord Mayor, urged Richard to send out troops after nightfall to attack the rebels, but, again according to Froissart:

> The wiser heads, such as the Earl of Salisbury, told the king: Sire, if you can appease them by fair words, that would be the better course. Promise them everything they are asking. If we begin something that we are unable to finish, there will be no stopping things before we and our heirs are destroyed and all England is laid in ruins.[40]

This advice was taken and Richard announced that he would talk to the protesters if they would assemble the following day, Friday, 14 June at Mile End. After riding there with a small retinue he met several hundred rebels who treated him courteously but demanded the heads of all traitors, the abolition of serfdom and a standard rent for land. But while he was at Mile End, groups of the mob entered the Tower where they ran amok, tried to kiss the king's mother and dragged out and beheaded the archbishop of Canterbury and other senior officials. They nearly killed Lancaster's son, Henry of Derby, an act that would have decisively changed the course of English history, but were persuaded to let him go. Meanwhile in the city at large, property was set on fire, there was indiscriminate killing and some 150 people known to be foreigners were murdered. They included 35 Flemings, chief of whom was the financier Sir Richard Lyons, and all were beheaded on the same block as a protest against the damaging competition of Flemish merchants.

The king, mostly on his own initiative, decided that he would deal with the crisis by meeting the rebels again the following afternoon at Smithfield, this time accompanied by men-at-arms and a number of lords, including Salisbury. A great crowd of rebels duly assembled near St Bartholomew's priory at Smithfield on the Saturday afternoon and they were led by Wat Tyler himself. Leaving his supporters behind, Tyler approached the king alone and addressed him in over-familiar terms, making grandiose demands such as the equality of all men beneath the king and the disendowment of the church. The several chroniclers who have provided accounts of this event then disagree about what exactly happened next but Tyler's insolence provoked men in the king's retinue to a violent response and he was killed. Most of the chroniclers do agree that Richard then – either in an act of bravery or extreme foolishness – rode alone among the rebels, saying that he was their captain now, and they were to follow him. This behaviour on the part of a slight, fair-headed fourteen-year-old boy had the desired effect of quietening the crowds and eventually persuading them to make their way home. In London the immediate threat of revolt passed and several rebel ringleaders were rounded up and executed.

But the revolt had long-standing roots in popular dissatisfaction with heavy taxation, penal labour laws in the wake of the plague, the repressive demands of a feudal society and the unpopularity in many quarters of a church increasingly seen as venal and corrupt, as well as the dislike felt by many for overmighty lords, such as Lancaster. The events in London sparked widespread revolts throughout eastern England, often targeting ecclesiastical centres such as Bury St Edmund's, Cambridge, St Albans, Ipswich and Norwich. Even in the North, there were attacks on clerical properties in Beverley and York. The East Anglian revolt was chiefly put down by Henry Despenser, the soldierly bishop of Norwich, who defeated a rebel force at North Walsham late in June: after this the unrest in the countryside gradually subsided.

The king revoked the promises he had made to the rebels under duress and justices throughout the kingdom were encouraged to punish malefactors with the full rigour of the law. Salisbury's ancestral lands in the West Country were not seriously affected by revolt. There was a minor rising in Bridgwater on 19 June and again it was the local Augustinian priory that was attacked, along with the manor of a prosperous local merchant, while in Ilchester the gaol was broken into and an unpopular prisoner put to death. Salisbury was one of the justices who dealt with disturbances in Dorset and Wiltshire and in 1382 he was appointed custodian of the Isle of Wight and its castle at Carisbrooke for one year and a justice of the peace responsible for dealing with any social disturbances on the Island, or in any part of Somerset, Dorset and Wiltshire.[41] The fact that Salisbury was regarded at this time as a major influence is shown by the fact that when a commission was set up in the second half of 1381 to 'survey and reform' the king's household, Salisbury was appointed a member along with the Duke of Lancaster, the two archbishops, four other bishops and four earls.[42]

Family tragedy and quarrels, 1381-1390

Disaster struck the house of Montagu on 6 August 1382 when Salisbury accidentally killed his only son, William, in a tilting bout at a tournament at Windsor. We have no details concerning how this appalling incident occurred, but it was a tragedy for the earl and his wife Elizabeth because, although they had two daughters, William was the heir to the Salisbury earldom and its rich inheritance. The earl was 54 years old and he had married Elizabeth Mohun around 1350 when she was aged about fifteen, so their son was probably in his late twenties. In 1378 he had married Elizabeth Fitzalan, the daughter of the Earl of Arundel, but no children had yet been born to them. The earl was so distraught at the death of his son that he ordered a brass plaque commemorating him to be placed in churches 'wherever he held lands' and one of these can still be seen in the church of All Saints in Calbourne, on the Isle of Wight.[43]

The young William's untimely death meant that Salisbury's heir was now his younger brother, John, born around 1330. When he was about ten in 1340 Edward III and his father arranged a very advantageous marriage for John with Margaret of Monthermer. She was the only child and heiress of the second Lord Monthermer, himself a first cousin of the king because his mother, Joan of Acre, was a daughter of Edward I. Margaret's father died from wounds received at Sluys in the year of their marriage and John inherited the barony and its estates as third Lord Monthermer in right of his wife.

John accompanied his elder brother on the Crécy campaign in 1346 and was knighted with him by the king on arrival at La Hogue. He fought in his brother's retinue at Crécy and under Prince Edward at the siege of Calais. After this his career lay mostly with the forces of Prince Edward, fighting under him in the campaigns of 1355, 1356 and 1359

The worst family tragedy to befall the Montagus occurred in 1382 when the second Earl of Salisbury killed his only son and heir by accident while jousting. He arranged for a brass plaque in memory of his son to be installed in every church on his lands, and this one, at All Saints Calbourne, on the Isle of Wight, is the only one which has survived.

and being rewarded with an annuity of 100 marks in 1357, the year in which he was summoned to parliament as a baron. This has led him to be described as 'Lord John Montagu', a title which is not to be confused with the barony held by his brother. After Prince Edward's death in 1376 he secured a place in the household of the young King Richard and was appointed a banneret in 1378. When Richard married Anne of Bohemia in 1381 he was one of three members of the household chosen to receive her on arrival and in 1381 he was appointed to the important and influential position of steward of the royal household, which he held until 1386.[44] Relations between the second earl and his brother were very good up to this point and John's success and advancement in his career had no doubt been partly owing to the high regard in which the second earl was held both by Edward III and Richard II.

Unfortunately, in the same year that his brother became his heir, Salisbury and John Montagu began a serious disagreement which developed into a bitter quarrel which lasted for many years. On 2 December 1382 Salisbury entered into a major commercial agreement with his brother involving a bond of £10,000, which was formally registered as a legal contract before William Walworth, Mayor of the Staple. In due course it became clear that John Montagu did not intend to pay his debts under this agreement and as £10,000 was a vast sum it caused a major rift between the brothers and Salisbury was forced to resort to legal action.[45]

The case was heard, on and off, for a period of seven years, in the Court of Chivalry, presided over by the constable and the marshal of England. This court developed in the second half of the fourteenth century as the place where disputes could be settled that arose out of the conflicts of war and were beyond the reach of the ordinary common law. In the first hearing of the case in 1382 the court found in favour of the earl, but John, who was by then steward of Richard II's household, appealed in November 1384. The presiding officer, as Constable of England, was the king's uncle, the Duke of Gloucester, and other members of the commission included royal favourites such as Robert de Vere. It would seem that they were reluctant to find against the steward of the royal household and allowed the appeal to drag on. Special commissions were appointed to deal with the case and in 1387 Gloucester found against John Montagu and ordered him to pay costs, which he did in 1388. John died in 1390 to be succeeded by his son, also John, who formally accepted defeat in this case in 1391. The result of this long-standing feud within the Montagu family, which was carried out in public at the highest levels, was that the second earl became entirely disaffected from both his brother and his nephew and determined that, though they might inevitably be the heirs to his title, they would inherit as little as possible from his estate.

Having played a significant role as an adviser to the young king during the revolt of 1381, Salisbury did not follow this up by playing an important part in the events of the reign as they gradually unfolded. Clearly the fact that he was in dispute with his brother, the steward of Richard's household, was an embarrassment, but the main reason is that, as he grew up, Richard II began to surround himself with advisers who were more of his own generation. In 1382, when they were both sixteen, he married Anne of Bohemia, the daughter of the Holy Roman Emperor and King of Bohemia, Charles IV. It was a happy marriage and they were devoted to each other but she bore him no children before she died, a victim of the plague, twelve years later. While they were married Richard often turned to her for advice and she sometimes saved him from foolish decisions.

Richard repeated the mistakes of Edward II by favouring young men who were essentially upstarts and one of these was Michael de la Pole, from a merchant family, whom Richard made chancellor in 1383 and Earl of Suffolk in 1385. Richard's closest favourite was Robert de Vere, Earl of Oxford, who did spring from aristocratic stock but was not respected for either good sense or personality. When Richard created him Duke of Ireland in 1386, this promotion was not well received because up to this time the rank of duke – which was rare in any case – had been restricted to members of the royal family. But Richard was developing a very grand concept of what a monarch should be. He had married an emperor's daughter and he began to see himself in a quasi-imperial role, set apart from even his most distinguished subjects and elevated to a high plane where reverence, obedience and magnificence were the order of the day.

Richard's first involvement in the French war was caused by the so-called 'Great Schism' in the western Christian Church which threw most of Europe into religious crisis and confusion between 1378 and

1417. From 1309 to 1377 seven successive popes resided in an impressive palace on the small papal estate centred on Avignon, in France, rather than in Rome. All of them were French and tended to be pro-French in their political dealings. In 1378 Gregory XI returned to Rome but died there the following year as a result of which cardinals in Rome elected Urban VI, an Italian, as his successor but a minority of French cardinals elected a Frenchman, Clement VII, who stayed on in Avignon. Both claimed to be the legitimate pope and Christian rulers were faced with the awkward decision of which pope to recognize.

The English naturally chose to support Urban VI, while the French supported Clement VII and Richard II re-opened hostilities against France by sending the bishop of Norwich (Henry Despenser) to Flanders on a 'crusade' against the supporters of Clement VII. This was popular with the Commons in parliament because it might strike a blow against Flemish merchants and because the church paid for much of the cost of the expedition. Landing at Calais in May 1383 Despenser captured a few neighbouring towns but failed to take Ypres and was faced with a large army under France's new king, Charles VI, who at the age of fourteen was even younger than Richard II. Despenser's army decided not to risk a fight and most men were back in England by October, with little accomplished. Richard reacted to this disappointment by resuming hostilities against Scotland, a formal ally of France. He personally led an army up to Berwick in 1385 but did not succeed in forcing a fight with the Scots and returned empty-handed.

By now the Duke of Lancaster was disillusioned with his headstrong and arrogant nephew and after several disagreements with him, he left England in order to pursue his claims to the throne of Castile. Rightly or wrongly he suspected a plot to assassinate him in England planned by the king's young friends led by the Earl of Oxford and possibly including Salisbury's nephew, John Montagu.[46] Lancaster's departure left Richard's two remaining uncles, Edmund of Langley, Earl of Cambridge and Thomas of Woodstock, Earl of Buckingham, who Richard created Duke of York and Duke of Gloucester respectively around 1385. Gloucester, in particular, was critical of his nephew's policies, as was the Earl of Arundel. When Richard's favourite, Suffolk, as chancellor, demanded higher taxes from parliament in 1386 the Commons refused to pay until he had been dismissed. This led to a major confrontation between Richard and his critics in which he eventually had to back down and dismiss Suffolk. Incensed by this affront to his regal dignity, Richard went up to the North where he attempted to establish a power base in Cheshire with the help of his friend Robert de Vere.

On returning to London the king was faced with an 'appeal' or accusation of treason against his favourites Suffolk and de Vere as well as others, made by Gloucester and the earls of Arundel and Warwick. Supported by the earls of Nottingham and Derby they confronted de Vere at Radcot Bridge in December 1387, defeated his northern troops and forced him to flee the country. Now known as 'the Lords Appellant', the five critics of the king dominated the parliament of February 1388 which sentenced Suffolk and de Vere to death in their absence and executed a number of Richard's lesser supporters, including his former tutor, Sir Simon Burley. Hence the young king had been put firmly in his place by a group of great magnates, but he did not forget the insults and indignities.

The Duke of Lancaster returned to England in 1389 having failed to establish himself as king of Castile and he maintained good relations with Richard and helped him to govern peaceably for the next eight years. In 1396 Richard concluded a 28-year truce with France and married as his second wife Isabella, daughter of Charles VI of France – aged six – and the martial nature of Edward III's rule was considerably modified. During this time the king developed his strong artistic interests, completing Westminster Hall with its fabulous hammer-beam roof, patronising artists and in particular encouraging the development of the English language under the poet Geoffrey Chaucer, who was one of his court officials.

During these quieter times the Earl of Salisbury was employed mainly in judicial and diplomatic work. He served on an appeal commission in 1389 which arbitrated on a case from the Court of Chivalry as well as others and in 1390 he sat on a commission concerning trade with Prussia. Meanwhile he continued to sit regularly, year by year, as a justice of the peace in the West Country, and on a special commission for crime in Southampton.[47] He was also involved in an ongoing legal case concerning his loss of the lordship of Denbigh. As soon as Edward III was dead Salisbury petitioned the first parliament of Richard II in 1378 for restitution of the lordship, claiming that it had unreasonably been taken from him in 1354 and returned to the second Earl of March. In 1379 the third Earl of March successfully rejected Salisbury's claims on a technicality, but Salisbury tried again in 1396 and the matter was still in dispute when he died. It is interesting to see that, before he fell out with his brother, John Montagu represented the earl as his attorney in the legal proceedings of 1379 and 1380.[48]

The sale of the Isle of Man, 1392

After the death of his brother John in 1390 the Earl of Salisbury did not feel able to patch up the quarrel with his nephew, also John, who became the heir to his earldom. On the contrary he took a number of steps to reduce drastically the inheritance that his nephew would eventually receive. These included the sale of the reversion to the valuable Somerset manors of Martock and Curry Rivell to John of Gaunt for 5,000 marks and, more spectacularly, the sale of the Isle of Man.[49] The purchaser was Sir William Scrope, eldest son of Richard, Lord Scrope of Bolton, a former chancellor, and the price was 10,000 marks. Scrope, who was about forty when negotiations for the sale began in 1389, was a soldier and capable administrator who had fought loyally with John of Gaunt and served as steward of Aquitaine and keeper of Calais, Cherbourg and Brest. He was very ambitious and keen to develop a power-base in the north of England and saw the Isle of Man, with its kingly status, as a prestigious acquisition.

The second Earl of Salisbury had been Lord of Man for 48 years when the sale was eventually agreed in 1392 and the question arises as to whether or not the Island had benefited from his rule. Two years after the first earl died in 1344 the third Earl of Moray was killed at the battle of Neville's Cross in 1346 and this strengthened Salisbury's hand in a number of ways. Moray died childless, so there was for a time no Scottish claimant to the Island while the defeat of David II at the battle and his subsequent captivity in England reduced for several years the threat of Scottish invasion.

The first real crisis that the Island faced after Salisbury became lord was the Black Death and although there are no records of its effects on the Island, we have evidence of the devastation it caused in the hundred of Amounderness, essentially north-west Lancashire. A contemporary inquiry concluded that in the ten parishes of the hundred, which included Preston and Lancaster, 13,180 people died between 8 September 1349 and 11 January 1350. Three thousand of these were in Preston, another 3,000 each in Lancaster and Kirkham, 2,000 in Garstang and 800 in Poulton-le-Fylde.[50] These are high figures and if they were to be replicated in the adjacent Isle of Man, the mortality rate there would have been very great. Perhaps that is why to this day the Manx are very hostile to 'longtails'. On the other hand the Irish Sea might have proved to some extent a barrier to the disease and although there were parishes in the Island, there were no towns or even villages at this time.

When a later Lord of Man, Sir John Stanley II, sought to establish what the ancient constitution and legal customs of the Island were in the early 1420s, he was told by the two deemsters, or senior justices, that the origin of the 24 Keys was uncertain but dated at least from what they termed 'King Orry's days', which is generally taken to mean the reign of Godred Crovan in the eleventh century. The Keys were freeholders whom the deemsters called at the king's request in order to give advice and support to the king at meetings of 'Tynwald', an institution thought to have its origins in the tenth century. Hence the two Montagu lords would have inherited this ancient constitution with its well-established laws and customs.

Salisbury would also have inherited a strongly established church system headed by a bishop of Sodor whose diocese included the Western Isles of Scotland as well as Man. There was a cathedral on St Patrick's Isle at Peel and an abbey at Rushen and the Island was divided into about seventeen parishes, each with a small church, or 'keeil'. The appointment of the bishop of Sodor had historically depended upon the political events at the time until in 1134 Olaf I granted the right to the abbot of Furness. After the Treaty of Perth the Scottish kings claimed the right of appointment, disputed by the Manx clergy who wanted to elect their own bishop. The Montagus inherited as bishop a Scotsman called Thomas (1331-1348) who imposed a tithe on the herring fishery and a charge of twenty shillings on the churches of Man. His successor was William Russell, thought to be a Manxman, who was elected by the Manx clergy and consecrated by Clement VI in Avignon in 1349.[51] The second earl, who though Lord of Man at the time was still a ward of the crown, could perhaps have claimed the right of appointment but the

Manx clergy possibly saw their opportunity to stake their claim to the episcopal appointment. Russell seems to have been a good choice because he remained bishop until his death in 1374.

Russell's successor was John Donkan, the archdeacon of Down, in Ireland. He was Manx and was elected bishop by the Manx clergy in St German's cathedral at Peel. Returning from his consecration at Avignon he was captured and ransomed at Boulogne and it took him some time to raise the ransom, so that he was not installed as bishop in Peel until 1377.[52] He was a man of considerable ability and remained bishop until he was translated to the see of Down in 1392. During his Manx episcopate he had to deal with the crisis of the 'Great Schism' in the papacy and chose to follow the English king and church in recognizing the pope in Rome, Urban VI, while the Scots, siding with the French, recognized Clement VII, the 'anti-pope' in Avignon. Clement excommunicated and deposed John Donkan and replaced him as bishop in the Scottish Western Isles (Sodorenses) though Donkan remained bishop in Man only.[53] This has not stopped Manx bishops ever since from describing themselves as bishops of Sodor as well as Man. It is interesting to speculate what part Salisbury played in Donkan's decision, but it is very unlikely to have been taken without his advice and his very strong advice would surely have been to support Urban VI.

Salisbury made his own contribution to the ecclesiastical establishment on the Island by founding a priory at Bemaken in 1367 but his main contribution to the infrastructure of the Island was undoubtedly the strengthening of the fortifications at Castle Rushen and Peel, already noted. This work was needed to defend the west and east coasts of the Island from possible attacks from the Scots, the Irish, pirates in general and latterly the French. In 1377 they attacked Castle Rushen but it was 'manfully defended' by Sir Hugh Tyrell, according to the chronicles.[54] In 1388 the French supported a Scottish attack on the Island, led by the Earl of Galloway, but again, Castle Rushen held out. As we know, Salisbury had a great deal of experience both as a military and a naval commander: he had been present at many a siege in Aquitaine and other parts of France and he knew what made a castle strong.

Hence his determination to build defences that would successfully protect the Island seems to have paid off and it can be argued that through an ambitious, and very expensive, programme of fortifications at Castle Rushen and Peel Salisbury made his Island secure against external threats. In stark contrast to the endless attacks and counter-attacks of the Norse and Scottish periods, which brought misery to the Manx people, the Salisbury reign in Man was one of relative stability and peace.

Though it is unlikely that Salisbury spent much time on the Island, it is clear that he maintained an efficient and loyal administrative machine to govern it. In 1406 Sir John Stanley I inherited a system by which he was represented by a governor with a council consisting of a comptroller, receiver, water bailiff and attorney general, all of whom were appointed by the lord. Their duties were to maintain the lord's rights and to collect the revenues that were due to him. The Island was divided for administrative purpose into six sheadings, each under the control of an officer called a 'coroner', who had assistants, called lockmen, in each parish. There was also a 'captain of the parish', who was responsible for organizing local militias. The only surviving documentary evidence we have of Salisbury's administrative activity is that he appointed a receiver in 1371 and in 1381 granted rents on the Island worth £40 to one of his retainers but even this fragmentary record is enough to suggest that the administrative system inherited by the Stanleys was long-standing and that Salisbury had detailed control over his Island revenues.[55]

The final issue is the matter of the Montagus' use of the title 'king'. As we have seen, there is no doubt that from the tenth century onwards, with occasional breaks, the Island was governed by kings who used that title up to the death of Magnus in 1265. When the Island passed to Alexander of Scotland in 1266 he seems not to have used the title 'king' but to have granted the title 'Lord of Man' as a courtesy title to his eldest son and heir. Had Alexander's royal line not died out, the Island would probably have become accepted as a natural part of Scotland and its semi-independent status might in due course have come to an end. It could be argued that it was Simon Montagu who resurrected the notion of a semi-independent Island by claiming that he had 'conquered' it from the Scots in 1301, bolstering this with the somewhat far-fetched notion that he had inherited Affreca of Connaught's hereditary right to the Island.

Bishop Anthony Bek was referred to as king of Man and when Edward II granted the Island to Henry Beaumont he specifically included the royal title. The earls of Moray do not seem to have used the title of king, following in the Scottish tradition of regarding the island as a feudal lordship under the crown rather than a semi-independent entity. However, when Edward III quitclaimed the Island to William Montagu in 1333 he specifically referred to royal rights and when Montagu took possession of the Island in 1342, he was crowned king by the Manx authorities, presumably the bishop or abbot of Rushen, authorized by the deemsters. Naturally, it was in their interest to preserve the notion of semi-independence for as long as possible.

The second Earl of Salisbury's high regard for the Island and pride in its possession is shown by the fact that, unlike his father, he quartered the three legs of Man with the Montagu arms and wore them on his surcoat in times of war and flew them from his pennants and banners, as shown by drawings in the armorial rolls. The ancient 'triskelion', probably a sun-symbol originating in Sicily as early as the seventh century BC, became firmly associated with the kings of Man during the thirteenth century and was used by Alexander III of Scotland after he claimed the Island in 1266. The earliest known representation of this symbol on the Island was carved on a stone cross found at Maughold and it is thought to date from the Montagu period.[56] There is no evidence that the first earl quartered the three legs with the Montagu arms, which suggests that the second earl took his association with the Island very seriously and was keen that others should fully understand that he was the Lord of Man and recognized as king within it.

There are no extant charters showing that he used the title of king outside the Island and this would seem characteristic of him given that he was not an aggressively flamboyant or self-asserting individual. The title may well, however, have been used on official documents on the Island and was in no way obsolete when Salisbury set his seal on the sale of the Island to Scrope in 1392. The latter, soon to be a strong supporter of Richard II and his 'imperialistic' ambitions showed no hesitation in proclaiming himself 'King of Man' after Salisbury's death, which probably made his unpopularity in England even greater than it was already.

John Montagu, third Earl of Salisbury, 1350-1400

Early life

The second Earl of Salisbury died on 3 June 1397, just before his sixty-ninth birthday. For the time, he lived to a good age and much longer than many of his contemporaries. In his will he left half his personal goods to his widow Elizabeth and the rest to the church and servants but left no disposable property to his heir. The will also directed that he should be buried in Bisham priory, which he had continued to support and maintain by the grant of estates and he left 500 marks for the construction of tombs there for himself, his son, his father and mother.

When he died seven years earlier, in 1390, Salisbury's younger brother, John, was not buried at Bisham, no doubt because of the fraternal quarrel. His will directed that he should be buried either in Salisbury Cathedral, where his son, Thomas, was the dean, or if he died in London, then in St Paul's Cathedral, near the font where he had been baptised. He directed that his tomb should carry the effigy of a knight bearing the arms of Montagu, with his helmet underneath his head. In fact he died out of London, so he was buried in Salisbury Cathedral, where his very fine tomb can still be seen. Ironically, it is the only tomb of these 'mighty Montagus' that has survived.[1]

His son John was forty-seven years old when he succeeded to the title and estates of his uncle as Earl of Salisbury and Baron Montagu and of his parents' estates and barony of Monthermer. This led him to quarter the relatively simple Montagu arms of three red lozenges on a silver background with the Monthermer green eagle on a gold background. Although the second earl had disposed of the Isle of Man and several valuable English manors, his successor was still a great lord, in possession of the remaining ancestral Montagu estates in the West Country and elsewhere as well as the acquisitions of his father. Also,

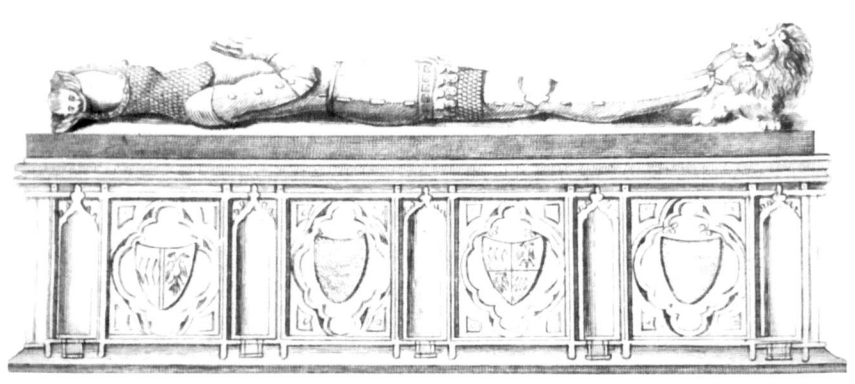

A drawing of the tomb in Salisbury Cathedral of Sir John Montagu (d.1390), the younger son of the second Earl of Salisbury and father of the third earl and his younger brother, Thomas, who was Dean of Salisbury from 1382-1404. Because of a family quarrel he was not buried at Bisham Abbey and, ironically, his is the only family tomb which has survived. (Robert Douch)

around 1382 Montagu married Maud, the daughter of Adam Francis, a former mayor of London, from whom she inherited estates in Middlesex. She was twice a widow and also inherited lands in Hertfordshire, Essex, Dorset and Sussex from her former husbands.

When he was nineteen, in 1369, Montagu went with the expedition of the earls of Cambridge and Pembroke to reinforce Prince Edward in Aquitaine and fought valiantly at the siege of Bourdeilles, in Périgord, after which he was knighted by the Earl of Cambridge. In the following year he was with the earls in their attempt to capture Belleperche, where he first flew his banner as a knight.[2] After Prince Edward's return to England, Montagu also returned and fought with his uncle Salisbury in his naval campaign of 1373. Well known to the Prince of Wales, Montagu served at his court until the prince's death and after that in the household of Richard II, no doubt helped by the fact that his father was steward of the royal household from 1381 to 1387.

In 1385 Montagu served with the young king on his somewhat fruitless campaign in Scotland but despite being a member of his inner circle he seems to have avoided becoming a target of the Lords Appellant during their quarrel with the king between 1387 and 1388. Although a man with considerable military experience, he was far more of an intellectual than most members of his family and in this respect he was a welcome presence at Richard's court. The king enjoyed literary pursuits and was surrounded by artists and writers such as Geoffrey Chaucer, Sir John Clanvow and Montagu himself, whose French poems, none of which have survived, were much admired by Christine de Pisan, the prolific Franco-Italian author of more than forty poetry and prose works.[3] In his biography of Richard II, Nigel Saul comments that the king 'enjoyed the company of men of a literary disposition: Clanvow was a friend, and Montagu possibly a close friend, of his. If a man can be judged by the company that he keeps, Richard deserves to be seen as a patron of letters.'[4]

It is not surprising that as a liberal intellectual John Montagu was attracted by the teaching of John Wycliffe (c 1325-1384), an Oxford don who became Master of Balliol College in 1361, Canterbury Hall in 1365 and Rector of Lutterworth (Leicestershire) in 1374. In a series of influential books he criticised fundamental aspects of Roman Christianity, including the wealth and secular activities of church leaders, the institution of the papacy, the insincerity of monks and friars, the ignorance of many clergy, the nature of the Mass (did the bread really become the body of Christ?), clerical celibacy, annates, indulgences, simony and many other time-honoured beliefs and practices. In 1382 Wycliffe produced an English translation of the Roman Bible, which made it more accessible to the less well-educated who could read English but not Latin. Wycliffe's followers were given the uncomplimentary nickname 'Lollards' or 'mutterers' by their critics, but they had supporters in high places, even as high as the Prince of Wales and John of Gaunt, both strenuous opponents of the 'overmightiness' of church leaders.

Around the courts of these two princes there grew a group of so-called 'Lollard knights' who, according to the chronicler Thomas Walsingham, were led between about 1372 and 1382 by John Montagu. They included John Clanvow, William Neville, William Beauchamp and a dozen or more others who mostly remained in high favour with Richard II, despite the fact that the 'Peasants' Revolt', which had been to a great extent anti-clerical made Lollardy seem a serious threat to established hierarchies. Walsingham mentions the fact that Montagu welcomed to his house at Shenley in Hertfordshire Wycliffe's scholar colleague Nicholas Hereford, who had worked with him on the translation of the Latin Bible, and that he removed several religious statues and images from his private chapel, in tune with the iconoclastic views of the Lollards.[5] Gervase Mathew, in his study of the court of Richard II, states 'the fact that [Salisbury] was a patron of the Lollards must have made him suspect among the strictly orthodox, but it also must have made him the leader of a section of opinion that was still otherwise politically inarticulate'.[6]

Despite the fact that Wycliffe did not really approve of the Crusading ideal, in 1391 Montagu obtained a licence to go on crusade in the Baltic, where for over a century the Christian order of Teutonic Knights had been in conflict with the pagan rulers of Lithuania. The fact that Henry, Earl of Derby, the Appellant lord, was also on crusade in the Baltic from August 1390 to March 1391 suggests that their enterprises were linked, as does the fact that others of the 'Lollard knights', such as Clanvow, Neville and Clifford were crusaders also.[7]

In 1394, reeling from the premature death of his much-loved wife in June that year, Richard II turned his attention to Ireland, where the landholders of English descent were under threat from the native Irish and had appealed to him for assistance. Accordingly he put together a large army of 8,000 men and sailed there in the autumn, remaining until May the following year. He managed to conduct a successful campaign which resulted in a considerable number of Irish chieftains accepting his overlordship. In his capacity as a soldier, John Montagu went with the king on this expedition, though he left before its conclusion in order to be one of four Lollard knights who presented a bill to parliament in January 1395 urging the acceptance of Lollard views. This did not please the king, who, according to Thomas Walsingham 'berated them soundly' when he got back from Ireland.[8] The following year Richard concluded a truce with France which was intended to last 28 years and which was sealed by his marriage to Isabella, the daughter of Charles VI. Unfortunately, she was only six years old, which meant that the king would not have a son for many years and would be deprived of the love and good counsel which his first wife had provided.

Supporter of Richard II, 1397-1399

Montagu succeeded to the Salisbury earldom in February 1397 and one of his first moves was to sell the castle and lordship of Wark to the northern magnate, Ralph Neville. Why he did this is not clear: did he need the money, or did he not wish to be responsible for a lordship which was in the front line of defence against the Scots? During the course of that year the king made up his mind to strike at the three lords who had humiliated him nine years before, namely his uncle the Duke of Gloucester and the earls of Arundel and Warwick. They were all arrested without warning in July and in the parliament held in September 1397 they were accused of treason by eight lords. Salisbury was one of these, together with the earls of Somerset, Nottingham, Huntingdon, Rutland and Kent, as well as Sir William Scrope and Sir Thomas Despencer. Richard had also gained the prior consent of his uncles the dukes of Lancaster and York for this strike, despite the fact that Gloucester was their brother. After a parliamentary trial, Arundel was condemned and quickly beheaded, while Gloucester, awaiting trial in Calais, was found dead, almost certainly murdered on the orders of the king.[9] The archbishop of Canterbury (Arundel's brother) was exiled for life while Warwick, who threw himself on the king's mercy, was condemned to prison for life and entrusted to the king's loyal favourite, William Scrope, 'king' of Man, who took him to his newly fortified castle at Peel.

Although a recent survey of the castle at Peel has found that major fortification schemes took place towards the end of the fourteenth century, it is not clear whether these were undertaken by the second Earl of Salisbury or by William Scrope, his successor as 'king'. The argument in favour of Scrope is that in 1392 he received a licence to repair the cathedral and improve the defences round it, while his father, Richard, Lord Scrope, the former chancellor, had for the last eighteen years been building a magnificent castle at Bolton in Wensleydale.[10] The military architect who worked for Lord Scrope at Bolton was John Lewyn and the younger Scrope would surely have been able to draw upon his experience and expertise. The argument in favour of Salisbury is that Warwick was imprisoned in an impressive tower which was already fully constructed by 1397 - only five years after Scrope's purchase of the Island. In fact, Warwick was Scrope's prisoner for only a year, after which he was moved back to the Tower of London.

Capitalizing on the success of the spectacular coup against his main enemies, Richard dispossessed them of their lands, which he distributed among his supporters, several of whom were also given titles with higher status. The earls of Nottingham, Rutland, Huntingdon and Derby became respectively dukes of Norfolk, Aumerle, Exeter and Hereford, while Scrope and Despencer became respectively earls of Wiltshire and Gloucester. The new titles and redistribution of lands had a major impact on the nature of the aristocracy and caused much upheaval as many old families were forced to relinquish their estates while Richard sought to break up threatening baronial power bases.[11]

It is notable that despite the fact that the Earl of Salisbury was one of the eight major supporters of Richard's strike he received no obvious rewards. He certainly did not become a duke, nor was he given any of the estates of the fallen lords. One favour that came his way was royal permission to sue the Earl of March in parliament for the return of the lordship of Denbigh, which the second earl had been forced to give up in 1354. In a case brought before the royal council in November 1398 witnesses, including a former esquire of the second earl and also his widow, argued that the second earl's written release of all his rights to the lordship of Denbigh was never actually delivered

This 'majestic' portrait of Richard II, which can be seen in Westminster Abbey, is one of the first realistic likenesses of an English monarch. It may well date from the 1390s, though it has been heavily restored since then.

and was still in the possession of the dowager countess. This opened up promising possibilities for a successful case but the death of the fourth Earl of March earlier that year meant that the earldom was held by a minor, his seven-year-old son, which made litigation very problematical.[12]

After the coup it seems that Richard's chief aristocratic advisers were the new dukes of Aumerle, Exeter and Norfolk and also Salisbury: indeed Froissart considered Exeter, Aumerle and Salisbury as 'especially in his favour'.[13] But the king was increasingly showing signs of paranoia, distancing himself from ordinary mortals and behaving with the sort of lofty arrogance associated with byzantine monarchy – which Richard admired, as his elaborate image in the famous 'Wilton Diptych' makes clear. Nigel Saul points out that the chroniclers describe how the king:

> was increasingly given to spending his time in the company of sycophants and cronies. The most regular attenders at his court now were the courtier bishops, household officials like Scrope and [the new dukes] – men who could be relied on to agree with him. He rarely summoned a 'great council' or turned to a wider circle of friends for advice.[14]

There was royal a council but after 1397 it came to be dominated by Sir John Bushy, the Speaker of the Commons, and Sir William Bagot, Sir Henry Green, the lawyer Laurence Drew and the cleric Ralph Selby, all men who would do the king's bidding without question. It is not surprising that increasingly critics began to see Richard's regime as a new royal 'tyranny'.

In the parliament that met at Shrewsbury in January 1398 the Duke of Hereford stunned the assembly by announcing that as he was riding between Brentford and London in the previous month the Duke of Norfolk met him and told him that the king was not to be trusted and warned him that he was still determined to avenge their defeat of de Vere at Radcot Bridge back in 1387. Norfolk was also alleged to have said that the king had the support of several great lords who were plotting their downfall, namely the Duke of Surrey and the earls of Salisbury, Wiltshire and Gloucester. Norfolk subsequently denied the charges and the king authorised a parliamentary committee to settle the dispute. It met in Bristol in March and decided, lacking clear evidence on either side, that the dispute should be settled in grand chivalric style by a trial by battle.

The king ordered that the contest would take place five months later, on 16 September at Coventry, though he made at least two unsuccessful attempts during this interval to persuade the two dukes to be reconciled. On the day of the contest and in front of a large and expectant crowd the king announced without warning that there would be no fighting: instead Norfolk was banished for life and Hereford for ten years. Although few contested the king's right to judge between two of his vassals, most sympathised with Hereford, who had loyally denounced Norfolk in the first place and whose ten-year exile seemed harsh. Whether Salisbury was indeed involved in a plot to bring down Hereford and Norfolk is difficult to say. The main problem for the king and his main supporters was the fact that Richard had no son and several of his relatives had a claim to succeed him, not least John of Gaunt. Although Gaunt had remained loyal to Richard, he was elderly and his heir, Hereford, was not someone they could trust. In this atmosphere of uncertainty it suited Richard well to have Hereford out of the country.[15]

Soon after Norfolk's exile had been announced, the king appointed Salisbury to the duke's former office of marshal of the realm for three years and in December he sent him on an important mission to Paris where he was entrusted with the receipt of the dowry of the king's young wife, Isabella. Richard also ordered Salisbury to do his best to prevent a marriage which Hereford was contemplating between himself and the daughter of a French royal prince, the Duke of Berri, by making clear at the French court Richard's objections to the marriage and also raising doubts about Hereford's suitability and character. Salisbury was successful in preventing the marriage but, as Froissart makes clear, in so doing he enraged Hereford by this affront to his matrimonial plans as well as his honour. Moreover, Hereford was not impressed by the fact that Salisbury spent a considerable time in Paris and returned to England without making any attempt to meet him. According to Froissart, Hereford's friends warned that:

> The Earl of Salisbury has done very wrong to carry such a message to France against the Earl of Derby [i.e. Hereford] and make so heavy a charge against the most honourable man in the world. The day will come when he shall repent heavily of this and say 'it weighs heavily on me that I ever carried a message to France against the Earl of Derby'.[16]

Hereford's dislike was no doubt further increased when the king put into Salisbury's keeping the manors of Trowbridge and Aldbourne which the second earl had been forced to relinquish to John of Gaunt several years before.

Everything changed on 3 February 1399 when John of Gaunt died, aged 58, and Richard took the fateful decision on 18 March to declare the vast Lancastrian estates forfeit to the crown and to extend Hereford's banishment from ten years to life. This was an extreme use of the royal prerogative and was widely considered a serious threat to the security of the landowning classes. Despite taking this calculated but very dangerous risk Richard then went ahead, with what in retrospect seems great foolishness, with a planned military expedition to Ireland, where the royal administration he had left in control in 1395 was under threat from local chieftains. He landed at Waterford in June and Salisbury, who had been sent to Scotland in March to conduct negotiations there, was chief among the great lords who sailed to Ireland with him.

Hereford, incensed by the injustice of the king's actions and anticipating the support of many of his fellow magnates, left Paris and landed at Ravenspur at the end of June with only a few men but was soon joined by the Earl of Northumberland and other lords. The king realized that he would have to return quickly from Ireland but he lacked enough transport ships for his whole army and accordingly sent an advance party under Salisbury to North Wales, a presumed loyal stronghold: but the Welsh refused to fight. Meanwhile the Duke of York, who had been left as keeper of the realm in his nephew's absence, marched with a force to Berkeley, near Bristol, where he met Hereford and agreed to support his cause, perhaps because he lacked the troops to fight him. Together Hereford and York marched to Bristol where the castle surrendered and Richard's men, William Scrope, Earl of Wiltshire, Sir John Bushy and Sir

Henry Green, who had all gone there for safety, were summarily tried and executed in Bristol on 29 July.

Meanwhile, the king himself arrived in South Wales on 24 July but was dismayed to find that there was no local support for his cause. By the end of the month he knew about York's defection and the fall of Bristol and decided to join forces with Salisbury in North Wales, travelling by night in the company of only a few lords such as the dukes of Exeter and Surrey, the Earl of Gloucester and a number of bishops. He met Salisbury at Conwy and we have an eye-witness account of their meeting. It comes from the pen of the French poet-troubadour Jean Creton who had sailed with Richard on his Irish expedition and returned in the advance party with Salisbury, to provide much needed 'song and merriment'. Writing in verse, he noted that both Richard and Salisbury were tearful and distressed and 'it was a piteous sight to behold their looks and countenance'.[17] When Salisbury told the king that he had failed to raise any support, Richard looked miserable and downcast. His position was indeed desperate because early in August the city of Chester, which Richard had considered his safest stronghold, had opened its gates to Hereford.

Richard sent the Duke of Exeter to Chester as an emissary but he was detained there by Hereford who instead sent the Earl of Northumberland to negotiate with Richard at Conwy. According to Creton, Northumberland offered peace on three main conditions: that Hereford's Lancastrian inheritance be restored to him, that Hereford would preside over parliament as hereditary steward, and that Exeter, Surrey, Salisbury and the bishop of Carlisle be put on trial for treason.[18] Well might Salisbury say, in Creton's words 'Now see I well that I am certain to be a dead man, for Duke Henry surely beareth a great hatred towards me...may Jesus, in whom I believe, vouchsafe to help us all.'[19]

After agonizing for several days and requiring Northumberland to take a sacred oath that Richard would remain king and unharmed, Richard left Conwy with Northumberland and rode to the castle at Flint. Hereford arrived there with his full army on 16 August and Richard, seeing the size of his force from the battlements, told Salisbury 'Now I can see the end of my days coming'. Salisbury's worst fears were realized when Hereford's supporters told him at Flint, 'Earl of Salisbury be assured that no more than you deigned to speak to my lord the Duke of

[Hereford] when you and he were at Paris Christmas-last past, will he speak unto you'. Jean Creton noted 'then was the Earl of Salisbury much abashed and had great fear and dread at heart, for he saw plainly that the duke mortally hated him'.[20]

At this point Hereford probably intended only to reclaim what was justly his, but as he moved south with the king and received support from all sides, he became more ambitious, especially when he was welcomed into the capital by the Londoners. Richard was put in the Tower and Hereford's mind turned towards how he might be legally deposed. As Richard refused to abdicate and only agreed to renounce his crown under duress, his deposition was hardly legal: but it was ratified by parliament which declared Hereford king as Henry IV and he was quickly crowned on 13 October. Meanwhile, Richard was taken under close guard to the Lancastrian stronghold of Pontefract Castle in December.

Enemy of Henry IV, 1399

Parliament met the day after the coronation and was soon told that the Duke of Gloucester had been murdered in 1397 by one John Hall, a prisoner in Newgate. He was brought in chains to parliament and confessed that he had smothered the duke in Calais on the orders of Richard II and the dukes of Aumale and Norfolk. He was condemned to the worst aspects of a traitor's death while parliament demanded punishment for six 'Counter-Appellant' lords. Henry IV decided to be lenient, so Aumale, Surrey and Exeter were demoted from duke to earl and Thomas Despencer lost his earldom. Salisbury retained his because when his turn came to defend his behaviour he claimed that he had only been an Appellant in 1397 at the king's command and that he had played no part in the murder of Gloucester. He also said that he was ready to defend himself as a gentleman if anyone did not believe him. At this point, one of Gloucester's former liege men, Thomas, Lord Morley, stated before the king and parliament that in his opinion Salisbury had been a double agent, pretending loyalty to Gloucester while supporting Richard and that he was actually the brains behind the 1397 appeal, not just a mere signatory to it. He then threw down his gauntlet and Salisbury did the same, whereupon parliament authorised the dispute to be resolved in the Court of Chivalry and Salisbury's punishment was delayed until it delivered a judgement.[21]

The Court of Chivalry met under the authority of the constable, the Earl of Northumberland, and proceedings opened in the great chamber at Westminster on 11 November. Both Salisbury and Morley were represented by counsel though they also made personal statements to the court. The fact that these statements were made in French reminds us that English was still some way from becoming the accepted language of official transactions or even converse among the literate classes. Morley repeated his accusation that Salisbury had been a traitor to the Duke of Gloucester, pretending to be an ally of his while plotting his downfall with Richard II and possibly his death. Hence Richard II was a tyrant and Salisbury was guilty of being his evil counsellor ('conseil covigne'). The court met again on 15 November and on the following day Salisbury launched into a detailed criticism of Morley's accusations, essentially claiming that they were all vague and riddled with inaccuracies and untruths. The constable agreed with him and required Morley to return to the court with more specific charges. This greatly angered Morley but he had no choice but to return to the court on 26 November with more details.

On that day Morley took the court back in history to the second Earl of Salisbury's contest with his brother in the same court, claiming that the present earl had gone to the Duke of Gloucester, at that time the constable, asking him to look favourably on his father's case and offering his services in return, as a result of which John Montagu (as he was then) signed up to go with Gloucester on a projected crusade to Prussia, though Gloucester never went. Hence, Morley claimed, Salisbury had been close to Gloucester since as far back as 1387. The court required a number of clarifications which took the case into early December when Salisbury rejected Morley's claims that he had been a major counsellor of Gloucester and again dramatically threw down his gauntlet in the court, whereupon Morley threw down his in return, demanding that a personal contest between them would allow God and St George to determine the truth. At the court's final meeting on 5 December the constable took Morley's gauntlet in his right hand and Salisbury's in his left, twisted them together and formally announced that there would be a trial by battle between Salisbury and Morley which was scheduled for St Valentine's Day, 14 February 1400 at Newcastle-on-Tyne.[22]

This promising spectacle never took place. Against the advice of many of his supporters Henry IV had pursued a policy of reconciliation with his former enemies. Some of them had lost titles, but not their lands or their heads, while Richard was still alive in Pontefract Castle. This proved to be a mistake because a plot to assassinate Henry and his sons and restore Richard was soon hatched by the demoted dukes of Surrey and Exeter, the demoted Earl of Gloucester, and by Salisbury himself, joined by a number of ecclesiastics and officials loyal to the former king. Henry IV's Christmas had been spoilt by food poisoning, but he planned to mark the Feast of the Epiphany (6 January) by a series of entertainments and tournaments at Windsor, where the plotters intended to strike. Someone – ranging from a prostitute to the Earl of Rutland – warned the king but despite the fact that the plotters knew they had been rumbled, they still rode to Windsor and proclaimed Richard II king.

When they realized they had no support Salisbury and Surrey fled westwards and reached Cirencester on the evening of 6 January. There they were surrounded by hostile townspeople and locked inside the local abbey. On 8 January they decided to start a fire in the abbey and attempted to escape in the confusion but they were caught by the locals, dragged into the marketplace and beheaded without ceremony. A similar fate befell Huntingdon, who was beheaded by a mob outside Pleshey Castle in Essex, and Despencer, who was beheaded by the locals in the marketplace at Bristol. The king presided over a trial of some ninety plotters at Oxford on 13 January, where most were acquitted on the grounds that they were pawns of their masters. Twenty-seven were condemned to a traitor's death but the king had most of them beheaded, though four suffered the full penalty of hanging, drawing and quartering. The chronicler Adam of Usk noted that what remained of their bodies were taken to London 'chopped up like the carcasses of beasts killed in the chase, partly in sacks and partly on poles slung across men's shoulders, where they were later salted to preserve them [for display]'.[23]

It seems that Salisbury's head was initially presented to Henry IV at Oxford, 'like fish in a basket' but the canons of Cirencester allowed his body (with or without the head is not known) to be buried in the abbey, where it remained until his widow received permission twenty years later to transfer it to the family mausoleum at Bisham. Whether Salisbury was a traitor or whether it was Henry IV who was the traitor is open to dispute, but Jean Creton had a high opinion of his fellow poet and wrote after his death:

> He was humble, sweet and courteous in all his ways and had everyman's voice for being loyal in all places and right prudent. Full largely he gave, and timely gifts. He was brave and fierce as a lion. Ballads and songs and roundels and lays right beautiful he made. Though but a layman, still his deeds were all so gracious that never, I think, of his country shall be a man in whom God put so much of good, and may his soul be set in Paradise amongst the saints, forever.[24]

Thomas Montagu, fourth Earl of Salisbury, 1388-1428

Rise from disgrace, 1399-1409

Thomas Montagu was born early in 1388, the elder son of the third Earl of Salisbury and his wife Maud and he was christened in the parish church of St Botolph in Shenley, Hertfordshire, with one of his godfathers being Sir Richard Stury and another Thomas of Woodstock, later Duke of Gloucester. This does suggest a close link between his father and Gloucester at that time, as Lord Morley had alleged. Either on or before May 1399, when Montagu was about eleven, he was married to Eleanor Holland, daughter of Thomas, Earl of Kent, Salisbury's friend and co-conspirator who was beheaded with him the following year at Cirencester. When his father was killed Thomas was twelve years old and he, together with his mother and younger brother and his wife faced a dark and uncertain future, with both his father and his wife's father judged guilty of treason.

    The government was prompt in rewarding the loyal citizens of Cirencester for 'executing' the earls and granted them all goods held by the rebels on the day of execution as well as two tuns of wine, four does and six bucks a year. An act of attainder was passed in parliament confiscating all lands Salisbury had held in fee simple (roughly freehold), and some of his property was given to other individuals. For instance, the Salisbury 'home' manor of Cassington, near Oxford, was granted to Sir John Cornwall, a knight loyal to Henry IV, and the king's younger son Thomas gained three pieces of valuable Arras formerly belonging to Salisbury: at the other end of the social scale the king's sergeant-at-arms, a skinner called John Colton, was granted the office for life of parker of the manor of Crookham.[1]

    Because of the act of attainder against his father Thomas did not become a ward of the crown in the normal way and he and his family were potentially left destitute. The king granted him an annuity of £100 in 1401 and in 1405 he and his wife were granted 'in consideration of the poverty of their estate' a further £100 from the revenues of the manor of Christchurch. In 1406 the chances of a reconciliation looked slim when parliament re-affirmed the attainder on Thomas's father and extended forfeiture to include all lands entailed to him on the day of his death. By now Thomas was eighteen and although there is little information about his life at this time, we must assume that he had, as a young man with slender means, served in the household of some great lord where he learnt the courtly and chivalric virtues and especially the ability to fight. In view of his later career it is clear that he was a natural exponent of the skills of a knight and this would have recommended him to his elders. It seems also that at some point in the first decade of the century Thomas went on a pilgrimage to the Holy Sepulchre in Jerusalem but fell ill on the journey and vowed that he would return later. Perhaps this journey was intended to be seen as a public atonement for his father's treason.[2]

Usurpers of thrones seldom have an easy time and Henry IV's reign was beset by rebellions. After Salisbury's 'Epiphany rising' Henry had little choice but to contemplate the disposal of Richard II in Pontefract Castle and by mid-February of 1400 his predecessor and first cousin had died, probably of starvation, at the age of 33 – the same age as Henry. The death of Richard made his young wife Isabella, daughter of Charles VI of France, a widow and after acrimonious disputes about her dowry she returned to France, a humiliation that endangered a long-term peace between the two countries. Henry also antagonized the Scots by taking an army to Edinburgh in August 1400 in the hope of enforcing acceptance of his right to overlordship, which he did not achieve. Soon after this the first serious rebellion against his regime occurred in Wales under Owain Glyndwr, a member of a Welsh princely family, whose quarrel with Lord Grey de Ruthin in North Wales developed into a full-scale national revolt which was not brought under control by the English until 1409.

On top of this Henry had to deal with the disaffection of his former ally, Henry Percy, Earl of Northumberland, and his son 'Hotspur'. Both men had supported Henry against Richard II in protest against Richard's elevation of their northern rival Ralph Neville to the earldom of Westmorland and they were rewarded by the new king with many estates, offices and titles. Not least among these was the grant to

Northumberland of the Lordship of Man, which was vacant after the execution and attainder of William Scrope. Henry's initial success in defeating Owain Glyndwr in 1400 proved only temporary and he called upon the Percies to take part in the defence of the North against the Scots and also Wales against the rebels.

In September 1402 the Percies won a major victory over the Scots at Humbleton Hill, avenging their defeat by a much smaller Scottish army at Otterburn in 1388. But Henry IV's order that they should not ransom their prisoners without his permission (because he was desperately short of money) together with a list of other grievances as well as a feeling that the king was weak while they were strong, led the Percies to enlist the support of Glyndwr and declare that the rightful king was the young Earl of March. He had a strong claim because he was descended from Lionel, John of Gaunt's elder brother, though through the female line. Henry and his eldest son, the Prince of Wales, raised an army and met Hotspur and his uncle Thomas Percy, Earl of Worcester, at Shrewsbury on 21 July 1403 where the rebels were defeated in a hard-fought battle and Hotspur was killed. Worcester was executed soon afterwards but Northumberland survived because he had not personally taken up arms against the king. Henry, the young Prince of Wales, was hit by an arrow in the eye which had to be pulled out – an agonizing experience which he was lucky to survive.

Two years later Northumberland rebelled himself with the support of the Earl of Norfolk and Richard Scrope, archbishop of York. They raised a force of 8,000 men at Shipton Moor on 27 May 1405 but disbanded after promises made in negotiations with the Earl of Westmorland, who then treacherously took them prisoner and handed them over to the king. The archbishop was executed, to the outrage of the ecclesiastical establishment, but Northumberland escaped and fled to Scotland. The king confiscated his estates and handed over the Isle of Man for safekeeping to his trusted Lancashire ally Sir John Stanley and in 1406 formally granted the Island to him and his heirs to hold as a sovereign lordship in perpetuity. The technical overlordship of the English monarch was emphasised by the requirement that Stanley or his heirs should provide two falcons at the coronation of Henry's successors. The Stanleys, created earls of Derby in 1485, proved very successful at retaining control of the Island, with short breaks, until the eighteenth century when the crown decided its autonomy was a threat to British trade and bought back the sovereign rights in 1765. That is why the sovereign of the United Kingdom is Lord of Man today, though the Island is not part of the UK.

Even though dispossessed of his lands in 1406, the Earl of Northumberland was not finished yet and in 1408 he collected together a force of lowland Scots and Northumberland men which invaded from Scotland but was defeated by loyal troops at Bramham Moor, near Wetherby, on 19 February. Northumberland died in the fighting and his severed head with its silver hair was subsequently displayed on London Bridge. The power of the Percies in the North was broken and ascendancy there passed to their triumphant rival, Ralph Neville, the Earl of Westmorland. Young Thomas Montagu was a natural fighter and it is more than likely (though unfortunately not documented) that he fought with some distinction in the royal forces during his teenage years, possibly in Scotland, in Wales and in the Percy rebellions. If so, this would explain why, when he reached the age of twenty-one in 1409, he performed fealty to Henry IV in June and was restored to all the estates that his father had held 'in fee tail'. Moreover, in October that year he was summoned to parliament as the Earl of Salisbury, marking his return to royal favour. Even so, he did not receive back his entailed estates at this stage, which no doubt gave him an incentive to serve the king loyally in order to have them restored in due course.[3]

The road to Agincourt, 1409-1415

Though a comparatively young man, Henry IV developed a serious malady from about 1405 onwards which became progressively worse and took the form of painful skin lesions and serious facial disfigurement. By 1409 his ability to govern had weakened and his eldest son took over many of his responsibilities, which resulted in some degree of tension between the two, especially when it was publicly suggested that the king should abdicate. There were also differences between them on how to deal with France, which in 1407 became divided by a bitter civil war. Just as later in the century the 'Wars of the Roses' in England featured a mentally incapable king and warring factions within the royal family, so in France the incapacity of Charles VI, who from 1392 suffered periodic bouts of mental illness, led to conflict between his younger brother Louis, Duke of Orléans and his first cousin John 'the Fearless', Duke of Burgundy, both of whom were ambitious to rule France in the name of the king, who was often confused and out of touch. In November 1407 Burgundy had Orléans murdered in the streets of Paris but the latter's young son, Charles, planned revenge with the help of many supporters, chief of whom was Bernard, Count of Armagnac, whose daughter he married. Hence the ensuing contest came to be considered a war between the Burgundians and the Armagnacs. As both factions were interested in gaining the support of England, this put Henry IV in a potentially powerful bargaining position through which he might strengthen and increase his own authority in Gascony.

The Duke of Burgundy in fact made treasonable overtures to Henry IV in 1411, offering him Dunkirk and other Flemish towns and help in conquering Normandy if Henry would support him against Charles VI. Burgundy is a confusing name because it describes both the duchy of Burgundy in France (today divided between four départements) and considerable territories in the Netherlands. In 1364 King John II gave the French duchy of Burgundy to his younger son Philip 'the Bold' who in 1369 married Margaret, heiress of Flanders, Artois and other territories in the Netherlands. Their son John 'the Fearless' therefore succeeded in 1404 as Duke of Burgundy and Count of Flanders, ruling what amounted to a 'state within a state' with its own considerable revenues and armies. During his lifetime John would use these, with Machiavellian ruthlessness, to advance his own claim to the regency of France and to secure more territory for his developing state of 'Burgundy'.

Prince Henry, whose youthful personal ambition was already leaning towards the reconquest of Edward III's possessions in France, was therefore a pro-Burgundian and urged his father to take advantage of this opportunity to weaken Charles VI but the king sent only 2,000 men to Calais which gave fairly minimal assistance to Burgundy before returning to England. This was the first English invasion of France for twenty-eight years and it raises the question of whether the term 'Hundred Years War' is a misnomer and whether one war ended in 1375 at the Treaty of Bruges, while another was just about to start.

In 1412 it was the turn of the Armagnacs to appeal to Henry IV and by the Treaty of Bourges they agreed to give back all the parts of France they had reconquered from the English since 1369 as well as

Gascon fortresses held by French garrisons, in return for the assistance for three months of an English force of 4,000 men. Prince Henry was not impressed by this offer but he and his father were not on the best of terms because the king resented his son's impatience and suggestions that he should abdicate in his favour. He therefore appointed his second son, Prince Thomas, later Duke of Clarence, in command of an army that landed in Normandy at the end of the summer of 1412. Clarence's namesake, Thomas, Earl of Salisbury, accompanied him on this expedition, presumably with his own contingent of men, and it took the form of a chevauchée from Normandy down to Bordeaux in support of the Armagnac cause. At this point the Armagnacs and Burgundians made a truce which left Prince Thomas and his army surplus to requirements. In November the English were persuaded to go home with a payment of 210,000 crowns, some of which might have found its way into the pocket of the Earl of Salisbury.[4]

Disagreements between Henry IV and Prince Henry over this campaign and other issues of government, as well as the prince's allegedly irresponsible lifestyle (no doubt exaggerated by Shakespeare) might have developed into a serious problem, but on 23 March 1413 the king died, to be succeeded by the twenty-five year-old prince as Henry V. As Prince of Wales he had campaigned against the Glyndwr rebellion for nine years and eventually defeated it, and he had fought with distinction in a number of battles against English rebels, notably at Shrewsbury. Fully aware of France's political weaknesses he was, like Edward III before him, keen to establish his own personal reputation and dispel the stigma of usurpation by at least winning back the Plantagenet lands in France lost since 1375.

From the moment he became king, Henry V worked towards putting his kingdom on a war footing, raising the necessary money for an army and persuading his countrymen, especially the aristocracy, to follow him to France. A great council in the spring of 1414 urged him to negotiate for a peaceful solution and ambassadors were sent to France for this purpose. It is a measure of the high regard in which the Earl of Salisbury was by now held that not only was he appointed by the king a knight of the Garter that year, but he led this mission to Paris, accompanied by the bishops of Norwich and Durham and three senior court officials. They offered peace and a marriage between the king and

Well-known images of Henry IV (top) and Henry V (below), neither of which is thought to be contemporary.

The Mighty Montagus

Catherine, the daughter of Charles VI, but at a high price. They demanded the payment of the outstanding monies from John II's ransom (said to be 1.6 million crowns), a dowry of two million crowns for Catherine and the grant of suzerainty over Normandy, Anjou, Maine, Touraine, Brittany, Flanders, Aquitaine and half of Provence.[5]

The French were prepared to concede some of these demands, but not all, and several further embassies, not involving Salisbury, met to haggle with them throughout 1414. Salisbury himself made a determined attempt during this year to restore fully the fortunes of the Montagus by petitioning the king at the parliament that met in Leicester for a reversal of the act of attainder against his father. He drew attention to many errors in the accusations made by the act and claimed that his father had been murdered without due process of law or judgement by his peers. The petition was refused, indicating that Salisbury still had work to do to prove his value and loyalty to the crown.[6]

In 1415, when his war plans were ready and the negotiations with the French had not resulted in an agreement that suited him, Henry V broke off the discussions and prepared to cross the Channel. In April Salisbury attended a meeting of the great council at Westminster which discussed final details of the forthcoming campaign and he indented to serve with forty men-at-arms, including himself and three knights and eighty mounted archers.[7] He set out with this contingent in the royal army of about 12,000 men which sailed on 10 August, landing in Normandy near the port of Harfleur, which was soon besieged. It fell after a stout resistance on 14 September, during which time the English army was significantly reduced in numbers by dysentery. Disappointed by this outcome, Henry V then moved northwards towards the security of Calais but was confronted by a large French army which blocked his way, near the village of Agincourt.

Despite the fact that by now he had only about 9,000 tired men, Henry V had little alternative but to fight, on 25 October, St Crispin's Day. The French made the same mistake as at Crécy in attempting disorganized cavalry charges across muddy fields against the massed archers of the English. About two thousand French prisoners were taken and Henry V controversially ordered them to be killed in case they escaped and regrouped. The French probably lost six times the number of the English in the battle and among the many high-ranking warriors who were taken prisoner were Charles VI's nephew the Duke of Orléans as well as Boucicault, the marshal of France. We know that the Earl of Salisbury and his men took part in this Agincourt campaign but have no details about his achievements, except that he survived, possibly having taken some valuable prisoners for ransom. He does not seem to have been paid what he was due for his military contribution to the campaign because thirteen years later he was still petitioning parliament for the money owed to him.[8]

Salisbury features in one of Shakespeare's most famous passages, Henry V's rousing address before Agincourt:

> Old men forget; yet all shall be forgot,
> But he'll remember, with advantages,
> What feats he did that day. Then shall our names,
> Familiar in his mouth as household words –
> Harry the King, Bedford and Exeter,
> Warwick and Talbot, Salisbury and Gloucester –
> Be in their flowing cups freshly rememb'red.
> This story shall the good men teach his son;
> And Crispin Crispian shall ne'er go by,
> From this day to the ending of the world,
> But we in it shall be remembered –
> We few, we happy few, we band of brothers....[9]

Unfortunately, Shakespeare's history is not always dependable. Bedford was certainly at Agincourt and so was Thomas Beaufort, but only as Earl of Dorset. He was created Duke of Exeter the year after the battle. Warwick and Gloucester played important roles at Agincourt and Salisbury was certainly there but his great achievements came afterwards and he hardly deserves a mention from the king at this early stage in his military career. John, Lord Talbot, does not deserve a mention at all, because he was lord lieutenant of Ireland at the time and did not fight at Agincourt. Following on from Salisbury's mention in the speech, a fine scene from the Laurence Olivier film of Henry V puts the king aboard a ship in front of a huge flag, flapping in the wind and emblazoned with the Montagu arms. One wonders whether the significance of this was appreciated by the producers of the film.

From Agincourt to Baugé, 1415-1422

The French historian, Edouard Perroy, reminds us that 'the campaign of Agincourt meant nothing decisive'.[10] Despite the fact that it was, and has remained, famous as a great English feat of arms it did not make Henry V king of France or end the war. On the contrary, after the battle the king beat a hasty retreat to Calais and crossed to the safety of England. Early in May 1416 the Holy Roman Emperor, Sigismund, made a state visit to Henry V, largely in an attempt to gain support for ending the schism in the papacy (there were then three rival popes). Salisbury, with the king's brother Humphrey, Duke of Gloucester, was given the honour of greeting him on his arrival at Dover, where it is said that Gloucester waded into the water carrying a sword and stating that he would deny the emperor entry if he had come to exercise imperial authority. Then, escorted by Gloucester, Salisbury and a thousand mounted men, Sigismund rode to London where he was lavishly entertained by Henry V for four months. Ultimately, Henry agreed to support the ending of the schism and the emperor in return promised support for Henry's ambitions against the Valois in France.[11]

Recovering from the shock of Agincourt, the French struck back by besieging the English garrison at Harfleur and the king sent his brother John, Duke of Bedford, with a fleet to relieve it, accompanied by Salisbury and his contingent. On 15 August, in the Seine estuary, off Harfleur, a naval battle was fought between the French and English fleets, lasting seven hours with high casualties on both sides. The French were beaten off, several Genoese carracks were captured, Harfleur was relieved and English control of the Channel was assured. In October John of Burgundy met Henry in Calais and offered to become his vassal and help him overthrow Charles VI, while the king also made treaties of alliance with the Hanseatic League and Aragon.

Confident that the cards were now all in his hands, Henry V made plans for a major invasion of Normandy, landing there in August 1417. Salisbury was with him and was immediately ordered to capture the fortress of Auvilliers, which he succeeded in doing, to be granted its lordship as a reward. Charles VI, backed by the Armagnacs, was in a difficult position, facing an English invasion in Normandy and a Burgundian army threatening Paris. He was not able to send relief to Normandy and as a result many of the fortresses and towns of lower

Normandy were captured. Caen put up a strong resistance, but fell on 20 September, and by the spring of 1418 Henry was in control of the duchy from Cherbourg to Evreux. In May Paris revolted against the Armagnacs and welcomed the Duke of Burgundy, who did nothing to prevent the massacre of about 2,000 Armagnac supporters. In January 1419, after a heroic defence lasting six months, Rouen fell to the English.

The Earl of Salisbury played a prominent part in these events, assisting the Duke of Clarence in the task of quelling resistance in lower Normandy during 1418 and capturing the towns of Harcourt, Courtaine and Chambrans, gaining the lordship of Neubourg as his reward in June. His role at the siege of Rouen was to take charge of operations against a group of defenders holed up in the fortified abbey of St Catherine and after the fall of the city he was instrumental in the capture of the fortresses at Fécamp, Gournay and Eu and the conquest of the county of Perche, an extensive territory lying between Normandy and Maine. On 26 April 1419 Henry rewarded Salisbury with the prestigious title of Count of Perche, a clear recognition of the important contribution he had made to the English military success so far, and he was also appointed the king's lieutenant general in Normandy.[12]

The devious career of John of Burgundy came to a sudden end on 10 September 1419 when, while conducting negotiations on the bridge at Montereau with Charles VI's heir the dauphin (i.e. the lord of the Dauphiné, a title traditionally held by the heir apparent to the throne), he was stabbed to death by one of the dauphin's men. This murder, whether intended by the dauphin or not, alienated much sympathy from his cause and Paris continued to support the new Duke of Burgundy, Philip 'the Good', so that the dauphin's sphere of influence became confined to the centre and south of France, where he chose Bourges as his capital city. Philip was twenty-five and married to a daughter of Charles VI but his policy was to continue his father's plans to increase the power of his semi-independent duchy of Burgundy at the expense of the Valois monarchy, and this meant alliance with Henry V.

The three main contenders to rule France (given that Charles VI was mentally incapacitated) had been John the Fearless, the dauphin and Henry V. The first was now dead and the second discredited by his murder, so negotiations during 1419 moved in the direction of Henry V marrying Catherine, the eighteen-year-old daughter of Charles VI, who would name Henry and his heirs as successors to the kingdom after his death: until this occurred, Henry would rule France as regent. This disinherited the dauphin, who was the eleventh child and fifth son of his parents: his four elder brothers were all dead and his parents, especially his mother, thought little of him and had been known to hint that he was illegitimate. On 21 May 1420 the agreements were embodied in the Treaty of Troyes, the city used by Charles VI as his capital, and sealed in a ceremony in the cathedral by Charles VI's queen, Duke Philip and Henry V. Henry and Catherine were then betrothed by the archbishop of Sens and a universal peace throughout France was declared. On 2 June Henry and Catherine were married in the church of St John at Troyes, an event at which we can probably assume the Earl of Salisbury was among the 'many English lords and knights, richly dressed, being in attendance'.[13]

Henry V, now in theory the regent of France, was welcomed when he entered Paris on the first of December, accompanied by many great lords, including Salisbury, who on Christmas Day was appointed governor of the territories of Alençon, Essay, Exmes, Bonsmoulins and Verneuil. Early in January 1421 Henry and his entourage rode to Rouen, the Norman capital, and according to the king's biographer, Christopher Allmand, 'this visit also gave Henry the chance to receive homages, including those of his senior commander, Thomas, Earl of Salisbury, for the county of Perche….homages which were rendered in the hall of the castle, symbol of ducal authority.'[14] By early February the king was back in England after an absence of more than three years.

Less than two months later disaster befell his brother the Duke of Clarence, who had been left in command of the English forces in France and given the task of subduing those parts of the country which remained loyal to the dauphin – who had not, of course, been a party to the Treaty of Troyes. Clarence embarked upon raids against the dauphin's lands in Anjou and Maine with 4,000 men but on Good Friday, 21 March, he was unexpectedly confronted at Baugé, near Angers, by a force of 5,000 men composed of pro-dauphin French and also a contingent of their Scottish allies under the Earl of Buchan.

King Robert III of Scotland, who succeeded his father in 1390, had feared that his young son and heir, James, might be murdered by rivals for the throne and accordingly put the eleven-year-old boy on a ship bound for France in March 1406. However, the ship was captured by pirates who turned the boy over to Henry IV for a fine ransom. A few weeks later James's father died and he became, in theory, King James I of Scotland. He remained technically a prisoner in England until 1424, though he was brought up and educated at Henry IV's court and remained on good terms personally with Henry V. In his absence Scotland was ruled by his uncle the Duke of Albany (who had probably murdered James's elder brother) and in 1419 Albany decided to intervene decisively in the Anglo-French war by sending a Scottish army of 6,000 men to France under the command of his son John, Earl of Buchan. It was now some of these men who stood alongside the dauphin's forces at Baugé.

On Easter Saturday Clarence, probably unaware of the true numbers of the enemy, unwisely decided on a surprise attack with a small force of 1,500 men and he ordered Salisbury to round up large numbers of archers who were foraging in the countryside and to bring them to the battle later. Having fought his way across a bridge with difficulty Clarence was surrounded by mainly Scottish men-at-arms and after fierce hand-to-hand fighting the heir presumptive to the English throne was killed, probably by a Scotsman, Sir Alexander Buchanan, who crushed his head with a heavy mace. Fortunately, Salisbury and his archers arrived in time to prevent the destruction of the English army, which he managed to regroup and lead eventually to the safety of Normandy. It seems that he took the survivors through thickly-wooded country to avoid capture and ordered that the doors from every village they encountered should be collected so that when they came to the river Loire they were able to avoid the well-known fords by the expedient of settling carts in the river topped by the doors, which made a workable makeshift bridge.[15]

Christopher Allmand writes that at Baugé Salisbury proved himself to be 'a commander of great worth and experience. It was he who prevented a rout and extricated the English from the dangerous military situation in which they found themselves. Henry owed much to Salisbury for his efforts that day.'[16] This contribution was recognized promptly when in May the English parliament formally annulled the act of attainder passed against Salisbury's father in 1400, which meant that he recovered not only a great many of the lands that had been confiscated but that he was restored to the social precedence formerly enjoyed by the first three Montagu earls.[17]

Baugé shook confidence in the ability of the English to maintain control and it gave heart to the dauphin's faction and encouraged waverers to change sides. Henry's response was to return to France in June 1421 with a fresh army of 5,000 men. He failed to bring the dauphin's supporters to battle but besieged the fortress of Meaux in October, where he received the cheering news of the birth of his son, Henry, in December. Meaux, battered by cannon, did not surrender until the beginning of May, by which time many of the English had suffered from the cold winter and sickness. By June it was clear that Henry himself was seriously ill and he died, probably of a form of dysentery, in the castle at Vincennes on 31 August, aged 36. His embalmed body was taken to St Denis, outside Paris, and then to Rouen where it lay in state in the cathedral before being carried on a bier pulled by members of the nobility to the castle, where it remained for two weeks before starting on an elaborate journey via Calais to Westminster Abbey where it was eventually buried, nearly nine weeks after his death.

Famous commander, 1422-1428

Charles VI died only seven weeks after Henry V, which drastically changed the political landscape in France. According to the Treaty of Troyes the nine-month-old son of Henry and Catherine, in addition to now being King Henry VI of England, was also King of France. Henry V had two surviving younger brothers, John, Duke of Bedford, born in 1389 and Humphrey, Duke of Gloucester, born one year later. Parliament approved the appointment of a governing council with Bedford as the senior member and he became regent of France while Gloucester, with the title of Lord Protector, supervised affairs in England. Given the history of these turbulent times they might have chosen to become 'wicked uncles' secretly disposing of the inconvenient baby king and then perhaps fighting a civil war between themselves to achieve power and the crown. However, they did not and instead loyally focused on the problems left to them by the premature death of their brother, whom they had both admired and respected.

The Treaty of Troyes was in many ways just a paper agreement because on the death of Charles VI the whole of central France and most of the south except for English Gascony recognized his son as the rightful ruler. He proclaimed himself 'Charles VII', but continued to be referred

A stained-glass window in Bisham Parish Church depicting Thomas, the fourth Earl of Salisbury, in full armour and Garter robes.

to as the dauphin by his opponents. Hence the task that faced Bedford was little less than the conquest of half of France and for this he needed the help of Burgundy. In April 1423 he concluded alliances with the dukes of Burgundy and Brittany, cementing these with a marriage between himself and Philip of Burgundy's sister, Anne.

Encouraged by the English defeat at Baugé, Charles VII assembled an army composed of his own supporters, bolstered by several thousand Scottish, Spanish and Italian mercenaries under the command of Sir John Stewart of Darnley. In the summer this force of about 10,000 men besieged the town of Cravant in French Burgundy which appealed for help to both the Burgundian and English authorities. They responded by sending to its relief a combined force of about 4,000 men, half of whom were English archers, under the overall command of the Earl of Salisbury. On the evening of 29 July Salisbury held a council of war in the nave of Auxerre cathedral in which he went out of his way to emphasise English respect for and solidarity with the Burgundian contingent in order to achieve a united aim among his troops. A number of proposals were agreed, chief of which were that the English and Burgundians were to form one indivisible army and that every man in each contingent was to live in harmony with the others. Two marshals, one English and one Burgundian, would control the discipline and movement of the troops, and any soldier who failed to maintain his position in the ranks would receive corporal punishment. Each archer would carry with him a wooden stake, pointed at each end, to plant in the ground in front of him for protection. On reaching the enemy's position, all those one horseback would dismount and fight on foot.[18]

On 31 July the two armies faced each other across the river Yonne, about four miles from Cravant, but neither was anxious to cross the waist-high river in the face of opposition. The Scots (who were the majority of the dauphinist army) began by shooting arrows and Salisbury replied by opening fire with his cannon as well as archers. Seeing that this was causing a lot of damage Salisbury personally led his main force across the river while another detachment under his second-in-command, Lord Willoughby, crossed by a bridge, where heavy fighting took place with Scottish troops. The bulk of Darnley's army retreated at this point but the Scots fought on and perhaps many thousands were killed or captured. Both Scottish commanders were killed and Darnley was taken prisoner. This was a notable victory for Salisbury in the first battle where he had been in full command and the fact that thousands of Scottish troops had fallen was perceived to be sweet revenge for the death of Clarence. The military historian, Alfred Burne, basing his assessment on a detailed account of this campaign by the Burgundian soldier and chronicler Jean de Wavrin, a member of Salisbury's army, has this to say about the qualities Salisbury displayed as a commander at Cravant:

> Thus we learn six things at least to explain Salisbury's military success. Notice first his successful efforts to weld together the heterogeneous elements in his army on the very eve of battle; the tact with which he employed exactly the same number of Burgundians as English; the sharing of the duties of marshal; the strict injunctions as to mutual behaviour. Notice next his careful foresight and planning – he thought out eventualities and was ready for them. Next, his care for strict discipline, doubtless inherited from his late master, [Henry V]. Next, his experienced eye, which told him that the French position was impregnable but that it could be successfully circumvented. Next, his dash and drive in hazarding a wide river crossing under the eyes and missiles of the enemy; and finally, the fighting spirit that he must have communicated to his troops that induced them to undertake what seemed such a hazardous operation.[19]

The Scots did not allow Cravant to destroy their spirit and the following year they sent another 6,500 men to France. Led by the earls of Buchan and Douglas they marched to Charles VII's capital city of Bourges where they joined forces with French and Lombard soldiers. The allies intended at first to relieve the town of Ivry, besieged by Bedford, but it surrendered early in August so they decided to strike instead at the English fortresses on the Norman border, starting with the most westerly one at Verneuil. They took possession of the fortified town by the simple ruse of pretending to be English, whereupon the citizens opened the gates. Bedford arrived with his army on 17 August to find the French, Scots and Lombard forces drawn up on open ground about a mile from the town and he assumed command of the part of his army that faced the French while Salisbury took charge of the division facing the Scots. Neither side wished to begin the fighting so both armies faced each other in the summer heat from early morning until 4.00 pm, when Bedford ordered an advance.

The English archers had difficulty driving their defensive stakes into the hard ground and the French used this opportunity to make a successful cavalry attack, which caused a degree of panic in the English ranks. Exceptionally fierce hand-to-hand fighting then took place between men-at-arms in Bedford's division against the French and Salisbury's against the Scots divisions, so that Jean de Wavrin wrote later that 'the blood of the dead spread on the field and that of the wounded ran in great streams all over the earth'. After about 45 minutes the French gave way and were pursued by Bedford back to Verneuil, leaving Salisbury's division still fighting the Scots. Bedford then returned and surrounded the Scottish troops who nearly all died fighting. More than 7,000 of the dauphinist army were killed, probably 4,000 of them Scots, while the English lost about 1,600 men in what some consider to have been one of the bloodiest battles of the Hundred Years War, a second Agincourt. Among the Scottish dead lay both Scottish commanders, the earls of Buchan and Douglas, and the slayer of Clarence, Alexander Buchanan.

Wavrin, to whom Salisbury was admittedly a hero, wrote glowingly of his contribution to the English victory:

> The Earl of Salisbury sustained the greatest brunt, notwithstanding that he wavered greatly and had very much to do to maintain his position and certainly if it had not been for the skill and valour and conduct of his single person in the midst of the valiant men who fought under his banner after his example very vigorously, there is no doubt that the matter, which was in great uncertainty, would have gone very badly for the English, for never in all this war did the French fight more valiantly.[20]

Verneuil was a massive blow to Charles VII, who was now very much on the defensive in his 'kingdom of Bourges'. In September and October of 1424 Salisbury joined with reinforcements from England under William de la Pole, Earl of Suffolk, in a campaign against the towns of Nogent, Senonches, Rambouillet and Rochefort in Champagne and was appointed captain of Nogent and Montigny. The following year, with Champagne secured, he led the drive into Anjou and Maine and on 20 July arrived outside the walls of the important fortified town of Le Mans.

Whereas warfare in the fourteenth century had been dominated by the 'chevauchée', or desolation of the countryside by a fast-moving army, the gradual improvement in the reliability of cannons meant that the fifteenth century increasingly saw the growth of siege warfare on a much greater scale. As a commander Salisbury was quick to realize the importance of new weapons and technologies and he already had a team of 80 oxen to pull his heavy 'bombards' as well as 3,000 pounds of gunpowder and 800 cannon stones. These guns were drawn up outside the walls of Le Mans and soon caused a breach which led the town authorities to negotiate for a surrender. Salisbury had the reputation of being a fair and chivalrous warrior but also a ruthless one if his adversaries did not play by the rules of war as perceived at the time. It was well known that in the previous summer the small town of Sézanne, in Champagne, had defied him and then been captured by assault. The penalties for this were harsh and they were fully exacted – the town was sacked, its walls razed to the ground, its garrison hanged, goods pillaged, women raped and citizens massacred. Le Mans wisely decided to offer the surrender of their town, recognition of Henry VI as their king and a payment of 1,500 crowns to the earl personally in return for being treated, as Salisbury promised, with 'courtaisie'.[21]

For this campaign in Anjou and Maine Salisbury issued a series of 'Ordinances' which give some insight into his strategy as a commander. He arranged for the army to be divided into 'fellowships' of five to seven men who could share the legitimate spoils of war between them but he also strictly forbade the plundering of the property of friends and allies. He also stipulated that each soldier should carry a stick about thirteen feet long which had a dual purpose; it could be used to make a defensive bulwark to protect archers, or it could be thrown into defensive trenches to assist their capture. As scaling ladders were so important in siege warfare, he gave oversight of their use to members of the gentry class, making them into an élite operation. He was also known to be generous in rewarding bravery by dispensing knighthoods and the grant of arms.

After the fall of Le Mans, Salisbury and his army moved on to Sainte Suzanne, where the effectiveness of cannon was described by the chronicler John Hall. He explained that Salisbury at first attempted to use his élite squads with their scaling ladders:

> And so the trumpets blew to the assault and scaling ladders were raised to the walls and the Englishmen with great noise began to climb and ascend....When the earl perceived that by this light assault and slight skirmish he lost somewhat and gained nothing he made a wall and cast a trench about the town and caused his great ordnance to be shot at that part of the town which was most feeble and slender and so daily and nightly he never ceased to beat and break down the walls and towers: and so that within two days the most part of the wall was pierced and cast down to the ground.[22]

In September 1425 the Duke of Bedford returned to England, leaving the army under the joint control of the earls of Salisbury, Warwick and Suffolk. Salisbury's role was to take charge of Normandy, Anjou and Maine, but in February 1426 he resigned his command and announced his intention to go on pilgrimage to Jerusalem in accordance with a vow he had taken in the heat of the battle at Verneuil, perhaps when the conflict was 'in great uncertainty'.

This unusual decision may have been prompted by personal animosity between Salisbury and Philip of Burgundy arising from the fact that Philip had made amorous advances to Salisbury's recently-married young wife, Alice, at a wedding party held in Paris in November, 1424: she was the daughter of Thomas Chaucer, Speaker of the House of Commons and granddaughter of the poet, Geoffrey. The English alliance with Burgundy had already been strained in 1423 when the Duke of Gloucester married Jacqueline, Countess of Hainault, who had angered

Philip by deserting her former husband, his cousin, and claiming back territory belonging to her that he occupied. She encouraged Gloucester to take a small army to Calais in October 1424 and occupy her disputed lands in Hainault, whereupon Philip of Burgundy attacked him in March 1425, causing Gloucester to flee back to England, leaving his wife to be imprisoned by Philip. Salisbury seems to have lent his support to Gloucester in this escapade, which did nothing to improve Anglo-Burgundian relations, which were already beginning to sour. Salisbury returned to England in February 1426 but after a few months he got cold feet about the pilgrimage project, successfully petitioned the Pope for a dispensation of his vow and returned to France in July, where he took charge of operations in Champagne while Warwick led an attack on Maine.[23]

Bedford returned to France in April 1427 and appointed Warwick lieutenant of Normandy, Anjou and Maine while Salisbury went back to England to organize the recruitment of reinforcements for the next campaign. He was appointed a member of the royal council where he was a regular attender for twelve months, from July 1427 until June the following year. Most of this time he was involved in the recruitment and equipment of fresh troops and he sailed with them to France in July 1428. He met Bedford in Paris and the decision was made to begin a knockout campaign against the dauphin's 'kingdom of Bourges' by attacking the city of Orléans, the richest city in France after Paris and Rouen and of great strategic importance because it dominated the river Loire and the routes to the North. It is likely that Bedford would have preferred more stealthy tactics but was persuaded to go for a hammer blow against the city by Salisbury.[24]

Salisbury began the campaign by establishing a base at Janville and then rapidly capturing the Loire towns of Jargeau, Meung and Beaugency, among lesser targets. He wrote to the Lord Mayor of London in August to say that he had actually captured forty places, 'some by assault, some by other means'.[25] He had equipped himself with some of the latest cannon, ordered from English foundries, three of them weighing 5,166 pounds per gun and capable of shooting a stone ball between 264 and 297 feet. He had four other cannon weighing from 4,700 to 5,350 pounds and 28 scaling ladders. In addition he had 48 fowling pieces, which were smaller guns which could shoot a projectile of about two pounds, and these were brought into use in between the shots of the larger cannon. Senior officers, it seems, were equipped with handguns, of which Salisbury had sixteen, with 1,200 lead pellets. In the opinion of Mark Warner, one of the very few people who have studied the career of Salisbury in detail, 'Thomas was thus no aristocratic numskull, amateurishly muddling along with tools a hundred years out of date; he was in fact a thoroughly modern and professional commander who kept abreast of technological change. In addition to this, he planned and conducted his sieges with mechanical efficiency'.[26]

Orléans was a fine city by the wide and fast-flowing river Loire, dominated by an impressive cathedral and surrounded by thick walls and defensive towers. Standing mainly on the north bank of the river, it was linked to the south bank by a sturdy stone bridge about 400 metres long, guarded on the south side by two fortified towers called 'Les Tourelles' which stood in the river and were connected to the south bank by a drawbridge. The commander of the Orléans forces, Jean de Dunois, made sure that the towers were heavily garrisoned and built earthwork fortifications on the south bank to guard them. Sending a detachment to capture the towns east of the city, Salisbury crossed the Loire at Beaugency and arrived on the south bank opposite Orléans on 7 October. The siege officially began on 12 October and initially consisted of regular bombardment from Salisbury's ordnance to reduce the morale of the besieged. On 21st an assault was made on the earthworks that guarded the Tourelles but it was beaten back. Salisbury then ordered the earthworks to be undermined and this led to a French retreat to the Tourelles on the 23rd. The following day Salisbury's men captured the towers and the French retreated across the bridge, destroying some of its arches to prevent pursuit.[27]

On 27 October Salisbury and some of his senior officers were in a room high up in the Tourelles and he was about to sign an order to the effect that as the city had made no attempt to negotiate for a surrender, it and its citizens would be subject to massacre and destruction in the event of a successful assault. As he gazed on the fair prospect of the town, perhaps with mixed feelings, a novice gunner among the defenders let loose a cannon shot whose explosion was heard by those in the tower and they ran to the other side of the room for cover. The stone ball smashed into the iron grille of the window with great force and part of the iron flew across the room and struck Salisbury on the side of his face, causing a terrible wound and gauging out his eye. He was taken to Meung for medical care and recuperation but he died there on 3 November, aged forty.[28] His body was taken back to England and a funeral Mass was held at St Paul's Cathedral on 29 November, after which he was buried at Bisham. His will left instructions for a chantry chapel to be built in the priory church at Bisham and also the construction of a tomb for himself and his two wives, four feet high. His late wife, Eleanor, was buried with him but his widow, Alice, later married the Earl of Suffolk and she is buried in the parish church at Ewelme.[29]

Jean Wavrin considered Salisbury to be the most successful and talented English commander of the previous two hundred years and he wrote:

> There were in him all the virtues belonging to a good knight: he was mild, humble and courteous, a great almsgiver and liberal with what belonged to him: he was pitiful and merciful to the humble, but fierce as a lion or a tiger to the proud: he loved men well who were valiant and of good courage, nor did he ever keep back the services of others, but gave to each his due according to what he was worth.[30]

Others agreed that Salisbury was a truly chivalrous knight. His contemporary Nicholas Upton described how many quarrelsome gentlemen came to the earl to ask him to act as an independent arbiter in their duels of honour, while the anonymous 'Bourgeois' chronicler of Paris wrote in his journal that Salisbury was not only a good man at arms, but also most chivalrous.[31] Nor was he without intellectual interests, as is shown by the fact that in 1426 he commissioned the English poet John Lydgate to translate a French religious allegory, the 'Pilgrimage of the life of man'.

Salisbury's death proved to be a disaster as far as the siege of Orléans was concerned. Had he lived it is more than likely that he would have used all his skill and experience to make the capture of the Tourelles and control of the bridge a way to bring the siege to a rapid conclusion, perhaps by a negotiated surrender, as at Le Mans. His death inevitably imposed a lengthy delay on operations and gave fresh heart to the defenders, who now destroyed the rest of the bridge, making a direct assault from the south more difficult. It was not until the middle of November that Bedford appointed William de la Pole, Earl of Suffolk, to take charge of the siege and he decided against an assault and instead built small forts (bastides) round the city to prevent access and thereby starve the citizens into surrender. A French attack on an English force bringing food to Suffolk's army (mainly herrings for Lent) was heavily defeated at Rouvray on 12 February 1429 and the future looked bleak for the defenders.

On the very same day, however, a young peasant girl called Joan of Arc persuaded her local lord that she had a divine mission to rescue Orléans and crown the dauphin at Rheims. On 9 March she was taken to meet Charles VII at Chinon and he was impressed and sent her to Poitiers to have her claims of divine voices heard by a tribunal of clerics. They recommended her to him and on 22 March she entered his service. She accompanied a relief force which entered Orléans on 29 April, where her extraordinary personality raised the expectations of the besieged to new heights. Over the next few days several English bastides were captured and finally the Tourelles were retaken on 7 May. Suffolk abandoned the siege the next day because the English could no longer control the supply route to the city and the French went onto the offensive and Suffolk was defeated at Patay on 18 June and taken prisoner. The French then marched triumphantly through Champagne, which had been strongly under the control of Salisbury during his lifetime and on 17 July Charles VII was formally anointed as king in Rheims cathedral. This was a crucially symbolic event which raised his personal prestige and greatly strengthened his claim to rule France.

The Burgundians managed to capture Joan of Arc on 23 May 1430 and handed her over to the English who had her tried as a witch and burnt at the stake in Rouen on 30 May the next year. Bedford followed this up with a formal coronation of Henry VI on 29 December in Paris and the war went on. An attempt at peacemaking failed at Arras in the summer of 1435 and this was followed by a decisive move by Philip of Burgundy who renounced his alliance with the English, recognized Charles VII as the legitimate king of France, and handed over to him the control of Paris. Bedford died in the autumn of 1435 and over

Thomas Montagu, fourth Earl of Salisbury, 1388-1428

The fourth Earl of Salisbury. Detail from a 15th century drawing in the British Library.

the coming years Charles VII drastically reformed his administration and his army, realizing the great importance of cannon and equipping his forces with some of the most effective artillery in Europe. In 1449 the French recaptured Rouen and defeated the English at Formigny.

With Normandy in his hands, Charles VII then turned to Gascony, the last vestige of England's French empire, and Bordeaux surrendered in June 1452. It was retaken by the Earl of Shrewsbury in October, but he was defeated at Castillon in July the next year, a battle that is said to have ended the so-called 'Hundred Years War', even though peace was not formally made between England and France until 1475. Even then, these two rival nations, which Jonathan Swift lampooned in 'Gulliver's Travels' as 'Liliput and Blefuscu' were constantly at war throughout the succeeding centuries and did not finally bury the hatchet until the French were defeated at Waterloo in 1815. Centuries of fighting between England and Scotland ceased much earlier, in 1603, when in an irony which might have had both Edward I and Edward III turning in their graves, James VI, King of Scotland, succeeded legally and peacefully as James I, King of England, thereby uniting the two ancient enemies under his personal rule.

Aftermath

The Neville earldom of Salisbury

The fourth Earl of Salisbury left two children, an illegitimate son called John and a daughter, Alice. Neither the identity of John's mother nor the date of his birth is known, but John was left £100 in his father's will with which to buy land. His illegitimacy debarred him from succeeding to the earldom or its associated properties and he made his way in the world as a freelance knight, often known as the 'Bastard of Salisbury'. Details of Sir John Montagu's career are sparse but it seems that he was captain of Argentan and Gournay in 1430, that he fought at the siege of Louviers in 1431 and was involved in action the following year at Bonsmoulins and St Cenery. In 1434 he served under the Earl of Arundel with six lances and twenty archers, in 1439 he fought with the Earl of Somerset and in 1441 he was fighting for the Duke of York. About this time he was described as lord of Montgomery, but according to Mark Warner, 'little if any hard cash would have accrued from this estate'. He was captain of Fresnay le Vicomte from 1446-8 and he is last recorded as taking part in the evacuation of Bordeaux in 1453.[1]

Earl Thomas's daughter Alice was his only surviving child by his first wife Eleanor Holland. Born in 1406 she was married at the age of fifteen to Richard Neville, a younger son of Ralph Neville, Earl of Westmorland, and his wife Lady Joan Beaufort. The important question after the death of Thomas was who should succeed to the earldom, because there were two possibilities. One was Thomas's uncle Richard, his father's younger brother, who had a claim by male primogeniture, while Ralph Neville insisted that the earldom should pass first to his wife and then to him as her husband. Male primogeniture was not at this time strictly enshrined either in law or practice and a meeting of the royal council on 7 May 1429 confirmed that the title of Earl of Salisbury would go in right of his wife to Richard Neville, while Richard Montagu (of whom little more is known) was granted some of the late earl's estates.[2]

Even though the act of attainder against the third earl was reversed in 1421 Thomas had found it difficult both legally and in practice to recover many of the Montagu lands and as a result his earldom was valued at only £750 a year, probably the poorest in England. The great lordships possessed by his predecessors, such as Man, Denbigh and Wark had all gone and Thomas never even regained control of the ancestral Somerset manors such as Shepton Montagu.[3] He had, of course, gained the county of Perche and other valuable territories in France, but these were held under the vagaries of a continuing war and it is impossible to say how valuable they were to him in terms of hard cash. He certainly had the reputation of being very careful in the management of his personal property and estates and this was doubtless the result of being reduced to penury and disgrace by his father's attainder at the age of twelve, from which low point he had climbed back to favour and indeed military pre-eminence through his own distinguished efforts.

Thomas's lack of a legitimate male heir meant that the 'mighty Montagus', a family which through six generations had proved to be high achievers in politics and warfare, were replaced by the Nevilles, a powerful clan very much on an upward trajectory. Richard Neville was now recognized as the fifth Earl of Salisbury and when his mother Lady Joan Beaufort (a granddaughter of Edward III) died in 1440 he inherited many of her considerable estates in the North. This inheritance was strongly resented by Richard's half-brother Ralph, the second Earl of Westmorland, which began a bitter feud within the family, already feuding with its traditional Percy rivals.

Henry VI of England grew up to be an ineffective ruler who, like his grandfather Charles VI of France, suffered from mental weakness. Eventually his government was challenged by his cousin Richard, Duke of York, who himself had a good claim to the throne. Salisbury supported York, who had married his sister, and York was made Protector of the Realm in 1453 after the king suffered his first attack of mental illness, perhaps brought on by the news of the English defeat at Castillon. York appointed Salisbury chancellor and captain of Calais but in 1455 the king recovered and dismissed York who rebelled and defeated the king and his army at St Albans in May. Fighting alongside his father was Salisbury's eldest son, Richard Neville, who in 1449 had become the 16th Earl of Warwick in right of his wife, Anne Beauchamp.

The king recovered his authority with the help of his formidable queen, Margaret of Anjou, and in 1459 York, Salisbury and Warwick fled the country after a defeat at Ludford Bridge. Acts of attainder were passed against all three of them and Salisbury and Warwick responded by landing with an army in Kent, marching north, collecting support on the way, and defeating the royalists at Northampton in July 1460. After this York returned from the safety of Ireland and was again appointed Lord Protector of England, supported by Salisbury and Warwick. Queen Margaret struck back in December by defeating York and Salisbury's army near Wakefield, where York was killed: Salisbury escaped from the battlefield but was captured and beheaded the following night. Warwick then challenged the royal army at the second battle of St Albans in February 1461 where he was defeated, though he managed to escape. Meanwhile the Yorkist cause was now led by York's heir, Edward, who defeated the royalists at Mortimer's Cross and marched to London, where with the support of Warwick and the Londoners, he was proclaimed king as Edward IV on 4 March. He and Warwick then marched north and inflicted a decisive defeat over the royalists at Towton on 29 March, after which Henry VI, his queen and his heir all fled abroad.

Edward IV was crowned king, the attainder against Warwick was reversed and he resumed his career as the sixteenth Earl of Warwick and sixth Earl of Salisbury and probably the richest man in the kingdom, as well as one of the most influential, enjoying an income estimated at £7,000 a year. However, the threat of renewed Lancastrian attacks was never far away, while Warwick and Edward IV fell out over the king's decision to marry a commoner, Elizabeth Woodville. This wrecked Warwick's plan to marry him to a French princess and filled the court with the new queen's ambitious relatives, who were influential rivals to Warwick. Over the years Warwick became more resentful of his decreasing influence and in 1469, having contrived to marry his daughter Isabel to the king's younger brother the Duke of Clarence, he raised an army and defeated the royal troops at Edgecote in July 1469. Edward struck back later in the year and Warwick, with Clarence, fled to France. There, having been a lifelong Yorkist, Warwick made an outrageously traitorous alliance with the exiled Henry VI and Margaret of Anjou and arranged a marriage between his daughter Anne and their son, the Prince of Wales. Warwick then staged a rebellion in the North and himself invaded from the South in September 1470 with Clarence, causing Edward IV to flee to the Netherlands, after which Warwick proclaimed Henry VI the rightful king again, with himself as the effective ruler of the kingdom.

But Edward IV was at his best in a crisis and with the help of Burgundian troops he landed at Ravenspur in March 1471, determined to

Aftermath

win back his throne. Queen Margaret and the Prince of Wales were in France gathering reinforcements and Clarence deserted Warwick and switched his support back to his brother. On 14 April Warwick's forces met Edward and Clarence at Barnet, where they were defeated in a battle confused by foggy weather and Warwick was killed. In May Edward defeated Queen Margaret's army at Tewkesbury, where the Prince of Wales was killed in action, while his father Henry VI was quietly murdered soon afterwards in his prison in the Tower of London.

The fate of Bisham Priory

Bisham manor and the house of Austin canons that was founded close to it by the first Montagu Earl of Salisbury in 1337 remained central to the family until the end of the fifteenth century. Unlike many great families, the Montagus did not make one of their castles into the primary family home and the fine manor house at Bisham, with a great hall dating from the period of the Knights Templar, was only one of their manorial residences, though it became firmly established as their mausoleum. In 1342 the first earl was buried in the priory church as was his widow, Catherine, after she died of the plague in 1348. When the second earl died in 1397 he left 500 marks in his will for the construction of fine tombs for his father and mother, his son William, whom he so tragically killed in a tournament accident, and for himself. His widow, the dowager countess Elizabeth, lived until 1415 and in her will she directed that she should be buried at Bisham and that a procession of twenty-four poor men, dressed in russet and bearing torches, should accompany her body when it arrived at the priory church. She also wanted her hearse to be covered with a black drape and adorned with five large candles and left £12.10s for the singing of 3,000 Masses after her burial. Finally, she bequeathed 500 marks to maintain a chantry priest and a secular priest to pray for her soul.[4] Over the years successive members of the family gave money and bequests to the priory church, which was enlarged and elaborated so as to be a fit resting place for the Montagu and later the Neville tombs.

John, the third earl, who was murdered by a mob in Cirencester in 1400 was initially buried in the abbey there until his widow, Maud, was given permission to move his remains to Bisham by Henry V in 1420: she was eventually buried with him. Thomas, the fourth earl, was entombed there in 1428 as was his wife, Eleanor, and his daughter Alice and her husband Richard Neville, the fifth earl, as well as Neville's younger son Thomas. Warwick 'the Kingmaker' was responsible for interring the beheaded body of his father and Thomas at Bisham and he also named the priory as his own place of rest, which was an interesting choice, given his Neville and Beauchamp connections. Also killed with him at Barnet and buried at Bisham was his younger brother John, elevated by Edward IV to the dignity of Marquess of Montagu as a compensation for being given, and then deprived of, the earldom of Northumberland. The Duke of Clarence's son Edward, Earl of Warwick, who was executed by Henry VII after the failure of Perkin Warbeck's rebellion in 1499, was laid to rest at Bisham as was Arthur Pole, the son of Margaret, Countess of Salisbury, who predeceased her in 1539.

As is well known, in the 1530s Henry VIII embarked upon a campaign against monastic houses and in 1536 the priory surrendered to the king as part of his first strike against lesser establishments. It was not immediately closed and in fact the king founded the Benedictine abbey of the Holy Trinity there in 1537, to which he moved the abbot and monks from the dissolved abbey at Chertsey. However, in the final sweep against the larger monasteries in 1538 Bisham Abbey, as it now was, surrendered to the king and was dissolved only six months later. When Henry VIII divorced Anne of Cleves in 1540 he gave her several properties, including Bisham Manor, which, at the request of Edward VI, she exchanged in 1552 for the manor of Westhorpe in Suffolk, the property of Sir Philip Hoby, an influential Tudor diplomat. His religious views tended towards Puritanism and in 1557 he decided to extend and improve the manor house at Bisham at the expense of the priory church, which was admittedly in a dilapidated and unused state. As a result the entire church was demolished and its stones used in the re-modelling of the main house, while the Montagu tombs were, it seems, broken up and dispersed. In Burghfield church, near Reading, there is a mutilated alabaster effigy which may be that of Richard Neville, the fifth Earl of Salisbury, but of the other tombs there is no trace.

Bisham remained in the Hoby family until the middle of the eighteenth century when it passed to the Vansittarts, who made their fortune in India. Death duties brought about the sale of the manor to the Central Council for Physical Recreation in 1965, since when Bisham Abbey has been developed into an impressive national facility for recreation and sport.[5]

Appendix

Later Earls of Salisbury

After his death at Barnet Warwick's vast possessions and many titles forfeited to the crown and the earldoms of Warwick and Salisbury were granted in new creations to Clarence. But this fickle man, perhaps unhinged by what he claimed was the murder of his wife, plotted against his brother in 1477 and was judged a traitor by Edward IV and executed the following year. The earldom of Salisbury was then recreated for Edward of Middleham, the son of Richard III: but Edward died, aged eleven, in 1484. The earldom reverted to the crown and it was granted by Henry VIII in 1512 to Clarence's daughter, Margaret, who became Countess of Salisbury in her own right. She married Sir Richard Pole, a cousin of Henry VII, and they had four sons, the elder of whom was given the (Neville) title of Baron Montagu. They were staunch Catholics and another son, Reginald, became a cardinal and a strong opponent of Henry VIII's marriage to Anne Boleyn as well as the Reformation. This, and the family's status as heirs of the Plantagenets, was too much of a risk for Henry VIII, and Lord Montagu was beheaded for treason in 1539 and his mother (at the age of 67) in 1541. An act of attainder was passed against her and the earldom of Salisbury reverted once more to the crown.

The title was recreated in 1605 by James I for his hard-working and loyal minister, Robert Cecil, whom he had already created Baron Cecil in 1603 and Viscount Cranborne in the following year. In 1611 Hatfield House, a vast Jacobean mansion, was completed for him in Hertfordshire and it remains the main seat of the family. The earldom passed down in the main line and was held by men of lesser prominence who engaged in politics with varying degrees of success, though the seventh earl was an important political figure who held high office in successive governments between 1780 and 1823 and was created Marquess of Salisbury in 1789. His son, the second marquess, also held high political office, while his grandson, the third marquess, was one of the great Victorian statesmen and prime minister three times, for a total of thirteen years, in the late nineteenth century. His son also held cabinet rank, as did his grandson. The sixth marquess contented himself with a military career and four years in the House of Commons, but the seventh marquess (born in 1946) has been a major political figure and cabinet minister. If the Montagu Earls of Salisbury were prominent national figures for several generations, it must be said that the Cecil earls have achieved at least as much, if not more.

The later Montagus

In the early 21st century there are many thousands of people worldwide who bear the name Montagu (in various spellings) and in Britain there are four holders of aristocratic titles who have a connection with the 'Mighty Montagus' of the fourteenth and fifteenth centuries. They are the Duke of Buccleuch, the Duke of Manchester, the Earl of Sandwich and Lord Montagu of Beaulieu. All of these have an undoubted common ancestor in Sir Edward Montagu (1485-1557) a distinguished lawyer in the early Tudor period who was appointed Lord Chief Justice of King's Bench in 1539 and Lord Chief Justice of the Common Pleas from 1545. It is clear that his father was Thomas Montagu of Hemington in Northamptonshire and his grandfather was William Ladde Montagu, also of Northants. Some genealogies suggest further that William Ladde Montagu's father was John Montagu, born c.1397 at Boughton Castle, Northants, the son of Thomas Montagu of Boughton, born in 1374, who was the son of a Sir Simon de Montagu, born in 1353, allegedly a younger son of John, Lord Montagu and brother of John the third Earl of Salisbury. However, according to the authoritative 'Burke's Peerage' it is more likely that William Ladde only assumed the name Montagu because 'he had some connection with the medieval family through inheritance or property' and it is not possible to prove the accuracy of the genealogy that links him directly to the Salisbury earls.[6]

Sir Edward Montagu was appointed by Henry VIII as one of the sixteen executors of his last will and as governor of his young son and heir, who succeeded him as Edward VI. In June 1553 his chief minister, the Duke of Northumberland, persuaded the dying young king to change the succession to the throne from his elder Roman Catholic sister Mary to his Protestant cousin Lady Jane Grey, who was married to Northumberland's son. Montagu protested that this was illegal but gave

Appendix

in when threatened by Northumberland. Edward VI died on 6 July and Jane Grey was proclaimed queen but after nine days general support switched to Mary. Northumberland, his son and Jane Grey were later executed and Montagu was imprisoned, though he managed to buy his freedom with a considerable sum.

In 1528, conscious of his family's ancestral links to Boughton, near Kettering, Sir Edward Montagu bought the manor, which had previously housed a monastic building, and constructed a fine house there. He married three times, but only by his third wife, Eleanor Roper, did he have children - eleven in all - and three of the boys became the progenitors of the aristocratic families which survive today. The eldest, Edward (1530-1602) was MP for Northamptonshire and he was knighted c 1570. His son, also Edward, was created Baron Montagu of Boughton in 1621 after loyal service as an MP under James I. His grandson, Ralph, the third baron, benefited greatly by supporting the succession in 1688 of William III, who created him Viscount Monthermer and Earl of Montagu the following year. He then married two wealthy widows and his son married the daughter of Queen Anne's close friend the Duchess of Marlborough, which resulted in his elevation to the grand status of Marquess of Monthermer and Duke of Montagu in 1705.

His son, John, (1690-1749) rebuilt Boughton House in the style of a miniature Versailles with impressive parterre gardens but he left no male heir and his titles became extinct on his death. Montagu House in Bloomsbury, the fine family residence in London, was bought by the government in 1753 as a home for the national collection of antiquities. In the early 1820s the original house was demolished and the present British Museum was constructed on the same site. The second duke's estates were inherited by his daughter Mary, who married George Brudenell, fourth Earl of Cardigan, who assumed the name and arms of Montagu and was created Duke of Montagu in 1766. This title became extinct on his death without male heirs in 1790 but his daughter Elizabeth married Henry Scott, third Duke of Buccleuch (pronounced Buckloo) and fifth Duke of Queensberry, who acquired her Montagu estates and assumed the surname Montagu Douglas Scott. The third duke's direct descendant is Richard Scott, the tenth Duke of Buccleugh, who is the owner of Boughton House and its magnificent art collection, now open to the public.

The title of Baron Montagu of Beaulieu (pronounced 'Bewley') was created in 1885 for Henry, the second son of the fifth Duke of Buccleuch, who was a Conservative MP. The second baron (1866-1929) was very interested in mechanics, engineering and motor cars, an enthusiasm inherited by his son the third baron (1926-2015) who became nationally well-known in 1954 after his arrest for homosexual activity, which he denied. His subsequent imprisonment led to widespread protest and the eventual decriminalisation of homosexuality in 1967. In 1952 he opened the National Motor Museum in the grounds of the family home, Palace House in Beaulieu, Hampshire, and expanded and developed it for the rest of his life. He was a major figure in the world of veteran cars, British tourism and heritage and after the hereditary peers were excluded from the House of Lords in 1999 he sat as one of the ninety elected members until his death in 2015. The fourth baron is his elder son, Ralph, a graphic designer and heritage journalist.

Sir Edward Montagu's third son, Henry, like his father, made his way as a prominent lawyer and bought the former castle converted into a Tudor manor house at Kimbolton, Huntingdonshire, in 1615. He was appointed Chief Justice of King's Bench in 1616 and then Lord High Treasurer in 1620, with peerages as Baron Montagu of Kimbolton and Viscount Mandeville. He continued in high office under Charles I, who created him Earl of Manchester (then a small but handsome Lancashire town) in 1628. His son Edward was a soldier who supported the parliamentary side in the Civil War and was in command at Marston Moor but later resigned under pressure from Cromwell, who considered him to be too much of a moderate. His grandson, the fourth earl, was a respected courtier of George I, who created him a duke in 1719.

His successors lived a ducal lifestyle at Kimbolton, which the architects Vanbrugh and Hawksmoor made into a fine Palladian house in the eighteenth century. The dukes played their part in politics as backbench members of the House of Lords and many of them had 'Drogo' among their first names as a nod to their ancient lineage. One of these was the tenth duke (1902-1977), who moved to Kenya where he farmed a 10,000 acre estate. During the 1950s he sold Kimbolton Castle and nearly all his other British properties to meet death duties and other debts and it was opened as an independent school. Subsequently the duke's business venture in Kenya failed and the family fortunes were reduced drastically. His eldest son succeeded him in 1977 but died without male heirs in 1985 to be succeeded by his brother, who tried his hand at a number of jobs before being imprisoned for fraud in Ireland in 1996. He died in 2002 and was succeeded by his son, the thirteenth and present duke. Born in Australia, he lives in the United States, pursued by paparazzi keen to gather details about his colourful private life.

Sir Edward Montagu's sixth and youngest son, Sidney, served as a backbench MP for several constituencies and was knighted in 1616. He was one of the members expelled by Cromwell from the Long Parliament and he died in 1644, having favoured the royalist cause, unlike his nephew, the Earl of Manchester. In 1627 he bought Hinchingbrooke House in Huntingdonshire, where he was MP for many years. Originally a nunnery, it had been bought for a knock-down price by Richard Cromwell, one of Henry VIII's officials responsible for the dissolution of the monasteries, and his son, Henry (the grandfather of Oliver), converted it into an impressive house.

Sir Sidney's only surviving son, Edward, supported Cromwell and was elected MP for Huntingdonshire in 1645 and also served in the Commonwealth's army before being appointed a 'general at sea' in 1656. He remained a great admirer of Cromwell but after his death realized that a restoration of the Stuarts was the only solution to the chaos which followed. He commanded the fleet which brought Charles II back to England from France in 1660 and was promptly rewarded with the titles of Earl of Sandwich (in Kent), Viscount Hinchingbrooke and Baron Montagu of St Neots. He remained an influential figure in political, diplomatic and naval life until his death in 1672 at the battle of Solebay, where his ship was destroyed by the Dutch with the loss of many lives, including his own.

His successors served the community locally as MP or lord-lieutenant but John, the fourth earl (1718-1792) was a major statesman, holding several high offices especially first lord of the admiralty in Lord North's administration from 1771 to 1782, during which time the American War of Independence was lost. He is also credited, slightly dubiously, with inventing the 'sandwich' by eating bread and meat to sustain him while gambling. His successors continued to serve as Conservative politicians and local landowners and John, the eleventh earl, is one of the elected peers in the House of Lords. He has also licensed the use of his title for a chain of sandwich shops in the USA. In 1950 his father bought Mapperton, a manor house near Beaminster in Dorset and this is now the family home after Hinchingbrooke House became a school in 1970. As for the many Montagus who do not bear an ancient title, the fortunes of many of them can be followed on the family website at www.montaguemillennium.com

Simplified chart of the heads of the medieval Montagu family

Drogo de Montagud – time of the Norman Conquest, 1066

By descent to

Simon, first Lord Montagu (c.1259-1316), m. 1) Hawise de St Armand 2) Isabella

and his son

William, second Lord Montagu (c.1285-1319), m. Elizabeth de Montford

and his son

William, first Earl of Salisbury (1301- 1344) m. Catherine Grandison

His brother Lord Edward Montagu m. Alice of Norfolk and may have killed her.

and his son

William, second Earl of Salisbury (1328-1397) m. I) Joan of Kent, 2) Elizabeth de Mohun

Had an only son, William, killed accidentally in 1382, and a brother, Lord John Montagu, d.1390, who m. Margaret, heiress of Lord Monthermer.

and his nephew

John, third Earl of Salisbury (c.1350-1400), son of Lord John Montagu, m. Maud Francis

and his son

Thomas, fourth Earl of Salisbury, (1388-1428) m. 1) Eleanor Holland 2) Alice Chaucer

Had an illegitimate son and an uncle living at his death, but the earldom and other family titles went to his daughter Alice and through her to her husband, Richard Neville.

Sources

Unpublished theses

Douch, Robert, *The career, lands and family of William Montague, Earl of Salisbury, 1301-1344.* London University M.A. thesis, 1950

Warner, Mark William, *The Montagu Earls of Salisbury circa 1300-1428, a study in warfare, politics and social culture.* University College London Ph.D. thesis, 1991

Articles, etc.

Benedictow, Ole, *The Black Death, The Greatest Catastrophe Ever,* History Today, Vol 55, issue 3, March 2005

Curry, Anne, *Thomas Montagu, fourth Earl of Salisbury,* Oxford Dictionary of National Biography, Vol 38

Drury McPherson Partnership, *Castle Rushen Conservation Plan,* June 2012

Goodman, Anthony, *John, third Earl of Salisbury,* ODNB, Vol 38

Gransden, Antonia, *The alleged rape by Edward III of the Countess of Salisbury,* English Historical Review, Vol 85, 1972

Gross, Anthony, *William Montagu, second Lord Montagu,* ODNB, Vol 38

Kelly, Alice, *Echoes of Manx History in Somerset Records,* Proceedings of Isle of Man Antiquarian and Natural History Society, Vol 4

Leland, John L., *William Montagu, second Earl of Salisbury,* ODNB Vol 38

Ormrod, W.M., *Man under the Montacutes, 1333-92,* in Duffy, Séan and Mytum, Harold, *A New History of the Isle of Man,* Vol III, Liverpool University Press, 2015
William Montagu, first Earl of Salisbury, ODNB, Vol 38

Prestwich, Michael, *Simon de Montacute, first Lord Montagu,* ODNB Vol 38

Warner, Mark., *Chivalry in Action: Thomas Montagu and the war in France, 1417-1428,* in Nottingham Medieval Studies Vol 42, 1998

Wilson, R.J.A. *On the Trail of the Triskeles,* Cambridge Archaeological Journal, Vol 10, No 1, 2000

Books

Allmand, Christopher, *Henry V*, Methuen, London, 1992

Baker, Geoffrey Le, *The Chronicle of Geoffrey le Baker*, trans. David Preest, ed. Richard Barber, the Boydell Press, Woodbridge, 2012

Barber, Richard, (ed.) *Life and Campaigns of the Black Prince*, The Boydell Press, Woodbridge, 1979

The Black Prince, Sutton Publishing, Stroud, 2003

Barker, Juliet, *Agincourt*, Abacus, 2006

Brereton, Geoffrey (ed. and trans.) *Froissart: Chronicles*, Penguin, UK, 1968

Broderick, George, (ed. and trans.) *Chronicles of the Kings of Man and the Isles*, Manx National Heritage, Douglas, 1996

Burne, A.H., *The Agincourt War*, Wordsworth Editions, Ware, 1999

Bryant, Nigel, (trans.), *True Chronicles of Jean le Bel*, Boydell Press, Woodbridge, 2011

Carleton Williams, E., *My Lord of Bedford 1389-1435*, Longmans, London, 1963

Compton, Piers, *The Story of Bisham Abbey*, Thames Valley Press, Bath, 1979

Curry, Anne, *Agincourt, A New History*, The History Press, Brimscombe Port, 2010

Davey, Peter, *After the Vikings, Medieval Archaeology of the Isle of Man, AD 1100-1550*, Manx National Heritage, Douglas, 2013

Duffy, Séan, and Mytum, Harold, *A New History of the Isle of Man*, Vol III, Liverpool University Press, 2015

Forester, Thomas, (trans.)*The Chronicles of Florence of Worcester*, Bohn, London, 1854

Froissart, Jean, (trans. Geoffrey Brereton), *Chronicles*, Penguin, London, 1968

Given-Wilson, Chris, *Henry IV*, Yale University Press, Newhaven and London, 2016

Jacob, E.F., *The Fifteenth Century*, Oxford University Press, 1961

Mathew, Gervase, *The Court of Richard II*, John Murray, London,1968

McKisack, May, *The Fourteenth Century 1307-1399*, Oxford U.P., 1959

Moore, A.W., *A History of the Isle of Man,* Vol 1, Manx Museum reprint, Douglas, 1977

Mortimer, Ian, *The Greatest Traitor*, Pimlico, London, 2004

The Perfect King, Pimlico, London, 2007

The Time Traveller's Guide to Medieval England, Vintage, London, 2009

Mosley, Charles (ed.) *Burke's Peerage, Baronetage and Knightage,* 107th edition, Vol II, 2003

Munby, Julian, et al. *Edward III's Round Table at Windsor*, Boydell, Woodbridge, 2007

Ormrod, W. Mark, *The Reign of Edward III*, Yale U.P. Newhaven and London, 1993

    Edward III, Yale U.P., 2013

Packe, Michael, *King Edward III*, ARK Paperbacks, London, 1985

Page, W., (ed), *A History of the County of Berkshire* in *The Victoria History of the Counties of England*, Vol 3, 1923

Perroy, Edouard, *The Hundred Years War*, Eyre and Spottiswoode, London, 1965

Phillips, Seymour, *Edward II*, Yale University Press, Newhaven and London, 2011

Rigby, S.H., (ed.), *A Companion to Britain in the Later Middle Ages*, Wiley-Blackwell, 2009

Sacheverell, William, ed. J.G.Cummings, *An Account of the Isle of Man*, 1858

Saul, Nigel, *Richard II,* Yale U.P., Newhaven and London, 1999

    For Honour and Fame, Pimlico, London, 2012

Seward, Desmond, *The Hundred Years War*, Robinson, London, 2003

Sumption, Jonathan, *Edward III*, Allen Lane, London, 2016

    The Hundred Years War, Vol 1, Penguin, UK, 1990

Williams, Ann and Martin, G.H., (eds) *Domesday Book, A Complete Translation*, Alecto Historical Edition, Penguin 1972

Ziegler, Philip, *The Black Death*, Pelican, London, 1970

Reference Notes

Pages 7-29

1. Thomas Forester, (trans.) *The Chronicle of Florence of Worcester*, pp104-105
2. Duffy, Séan and Mytum, Harold, (eds) *The Medieval Period, 1000-1046,* Abbreviated in future to 'MP'. p111
3. Ibid. p120
4. Robert Douch, *The career, lands and family of William Montague, Earl of Salisbury, 1301-1344.* Abbreviated in future to Douch. pp1,182
5. Ibid. pp1-3
6. *Oxford Dictionary of National Biography.* Abbreviated in future to *ODNB*. Vol 38, p766
7. MP, pp127, 8 and Mark William Warner, *The Montagu Earls of Salisbury circa 1300-1428,* etc. Abbreviated in future to Warner. p5
8. Douch, p16, Warner p6
9. MP pp128,144
10. Douch, p20
11. Seymour Phillips, *Edward II,* pp110,111
12. Rigby, S.H., *A Companion to Britain in the Later Middle Ages,* p262
13. MP, 129
14. Ian Mortimer, *The Greatest Traitor,* p18
15. MP, p131
16. *ODNB,* Vol 38, p766
17. MP, p132
18. Phillips, pp190,191
19. Warner, p7
20. Douch, p21
21. *ODNB,* Vol 38, p766
22. MP, 133
23. George Broderick, (ed. and trans.) *Chronicles of the Kings of Man and the Isles,* p f.50r
24. MP, p135 and Drury Mcpherson Partnership, *Castle Rushen Conservation Plan,* section 2.6
25. Warner, p8; Douch pp17,18
26. Warner, p8
27. Warner, p10, Douch, pp18,19
28. Douch, p21, Phillips, p274
29. Warner, p13
30. Douch, p11
31. Ibid. pp12-15
32. Phillips, pp318,319,355
33. MP, pp137,14

Reference Notes

Pages 30-71

1. Douch. Illustration of her tomb in the Appendix.
2. Phillips, p409
3. Ian Mortimer, *Edward III*, pp405-418
4. Douch, p37
5. Ibid. pp27-35
6. Ibid. p30
7. Ibid.
8. Ibid. p 71
9. Warner, p16
10. Geoffrey le Baker, *The Chronicle of Geoffrey le Baker*, p43
11. Ibid.
12. Mortimer, *Edward III*, p93
13. Douch, p96
14. Ibid. p51
15. MP, pp152,144
16. Douch, p123
17. MP, p153
18. Ibid. p155
19. W. Mark Ormrod, *Edward III*, p162
20. Warner, p17
21. Mortimer, *Edward III*, p114,115
22. Douch, p51
23. Ibid.
24. Douch, p47
25. Douch, pp70,71
26. Warner, p18
27. Kay McKisack, *The Fourteenth Century*, p118
28. Douch, p51; Ormrod, *Edward III*, p169
29. Jonathan Sumption, *Edward III*, pp30,31
30. Douch, p52
31. Ormrod, *Edward III*, p173
32. Douch, p55
33. Ormrod, *Edward III*, p138
34. *ODNB*, Vol 38, p774
35. Douch, pp132,133
36. Ibid. p174, O3, p135
37. Ormrod, *Edward III*, p 135
38. McKisack, p121
39. Warner, p19, *ODNB*, Vol 38, p774
40. Sumption, p35
41. Warner, p19
42. Mortimer, p462, note 29
43. Ormrod, *Edward III*, p176
44. Sumption, p25
45. *ODNB* Vol 38, p774
46. Douch, p56
47. Mortimer, *Edward III*, p156
48. Nigel Bryant (trans.), *The Chronicles of Jean le Bel*, p80

Pages 72-115

49	*ODNB*, Vol 38, p774	1	Richard Barber, *Life and Campaigns of the Black Prince*, p14; Ormrod, p271
50	Geoffrey le Baker, pp59, 60		
51	Douch, p58		
52	Ibid. p7, O3, p250	2	Ormrod, *Edward III*, pp280-2
53	Ormrod, *Edward III*, p232	3	Ibid, p290
54	Ibid. p237	4	Geoffrey Brereton (ed.), *Froissart; Chronicles*, p109
55	Ibid. p238		
56	Geoffrey le Baker, p66	5	Sumption, pp62,62; Ormrod, pp300-305
57	Castle Rushen Conservation Plan, section 2.6	6	Ormrod, Ibid.
58	Ormrod, *Edward III*, p251 and note	7	Ole Benedictowe, *The Black Death, etc; History Today* Vol 55 issue 3, March 2005
59	Ormrod, *Edward III*, pp262,263		
60	Douch, p108	8	Philip Ziegler, *The Black Death*, pp232-239
61	From Adam Murimuth, *Continuatio Chronicarum*, 231, 232, quoted in Julian Munby et al. *Edward III's Round Table at Windsor*, p180	9	*ODNB*, Vol 38, p775, Mortimer, p274
		10	Warner, p61
		11	Ibid.
62	Ibid. pp182,184	12	Warner, pp61,63
63	Douch, p108, Ormrod, p301 note	13	Ibid. pp66,67
64	Douch, p85, Warner, p45	14	Richard Barber, *The Black Prince*, p242
65	Douch, p80		
66	Warner, page 32	15	Barber, *Life and Campaigns*, etc. p52
67	Ibid. pp38,39, *ODNB*, Vol 38, p775	16	Ibid. p93
68	Ormrod, *Edward III*,, p600	17	Barber, *The Black Prince*, p139
69	Mortimer, *Edward III*, p192	18	Barber, *Life and Campaigns*, etc. p100
70	Ibid.p193		
71	Ibid.pp191-198	19	Geoffrey le Baker, p127
72	Michael Packe, *Edward III*, pp105-123	20	Ormrod, *Edward III*, p390
		21	Ibid. p420

Reference Notes

22	*ODNB*, Vol 38, p776	49	Ibid. p68
23	Peter Davey, *After the Vikings*, pp53,54	50	Ziegler, p191
		51	MP, p344
24	MP, p368	52	Ibid.
25	Ibid. p369	53	Ibid.
26	Castle Rushen Conservation Plan, sections 5.1 to 5.6	54	A.W.Moore, *A History of the Isle of Man*, Vol 1, p196
27	Warner, pp67,68	55	MP, p159
28	Ibid, p23	56	see RJA Wilson, *On the Trail of the Triskeles*, Cambridge Archaeological Journal, Vol 10, No 1, 2000
29	Mark Ormrod, *Edward III*, pp433,434, 438,442		
30	Mortimer, pp365, 366		
31	Warner, p23		
32	Ibid. pp23,24		

Pages 116-130

33	Ormrod, *Edward III*, pp320,321	1	Warner, pp46,48
34	Ibid, p571	2	*ODNB*, Vol 38, p741
35	*ODNB*, Vol 38, p776	3	Ibid. p48
36	Nigel Saul, *Richard II*, pp24,28	4	Saul, p361
37	Brereton, *Froissart*, p197	5	*ODNB*, Vol 38, p741
38	*ODNB*, Vol 38, p776	6	Gervase Mathew, *The Court of Richard II*, pp 168,169
39	Brereton, *Froissart*, pp216,217		
40	Ibid, p219	7	Chris Given-Wilson, *Henry IV*, p 664, note
41	*ODNB*, Vol 38, p776		
42	Saul, p81	8	*ODNB*, Vol 38, p741
43	Piers Compton, *The Story of Bisham Abbey*, p33	9	Saul, pp373-379
		10	Davey, p54
44	Warner, pp40,41	11	Saul, pp382,383
45	Ibid. p97	12	Warner, pp65,66
46	Saul, p134	13	Saul, p391, note
47	*ODNB*, Vol 38, p776	14	Ibid. p391
48	Warner, pp64,65		

173

15	Ibid. pp395-402		16	Allmand, p160
16	Warner, p84		17	Mark Warner, *Chivalry in Action*, p150
17	Saul, p412		18	Alfred Burne, *The Agincourt War*, pp186,187
18	Ibid. p414		19	Ibid. p193
19	Warner, p84		20	Warner, *Chivalry*, p153
20	Ibid.		21	Ibid.
21	Warner, pp85,86		22	Ibid. p160
22	Ibid, pp90-104		23	*ODNB*, Vol 38, pp768,769
23	Given-Wilson, pp 161-163		24	Ibid. p769
24	Warner, p106		25	Warner, *Chivalry*, p163
			26	Ibid. p164
			27	Burne, pp229,230
			28	Warner, *Chivalry*, p146
			29	Compton, pp39,40
			30	Warner, *Chivalry*, p166
			31	Ibid.

Pages 131-155

1	Warner, p114
2	Ibid. pp114,115
3	*ODNB*, Vol 38, p767
4	Edouard Perroy, *The Hundred Years War*, p231; Warner, p116
5	Warner, p116
6	Ibid. p118
7	Ibid. p116,117
8	*ODNB*, Vol 38, p768
9	William Shakespeare, *Henry V*, Act IV, Scene III, lines 49-60
10	Perroy, p239
11	Christopher Allmand, *Henry V*, pp104-109
12	*ODNB*, Vol 38, p768; Warner, p117
13	Allmand, p114
14	Ibid. p155
15	Warner, p154

Pages 156-166

1	Warner, pp200,2001
2	Ibid. p121
3	Ibid. p124
4	Ibid. p46
5	*The Victoria County History: Berkshire*, Vol 2, p24, Vol 3, p139, and Compton, pp65,66
6	*Burke's Peerage*, etc. p2742

Index of main items

Adam of Usk, chronicler, 129
Affreca of Connaught, 13,17,114
Agincourt, battle of, 138-140,148
Agnes, Countess of Dunbar, 52,53
Alexander III, King of Scots,12,13,114,115
Alfonso XI, King of Castile, 62,63
Algeciras, siege of, 62,63
Allmand, Professor Christopher, 142,143
Anne of Bohemia, wife of Richard II, 107,108
Aquitaine, 8,28,51,52,72,84,89,91,93,97,100,111,113,118,138
Armagnacs, 135,136,140,141
Arundel, Earl of, 109,110,120
Audley, Hugh, 25,28,47

Badlesmere, Sir Bartholomew, 26
Baker, Geoffrey le, chronicler, 40,43,55,58,88
Ball, John, 102
Balliol family, 9,13,14,41,44,45
Bannockburn, battle of, 24,28,42
Bastard of Salisbury, 156
Baugé, battle of, 142-4,146
Beaumont, Henry de, 23,41,43,114
Bedford, John, Duke of, 6,140,144,146-9
Bek, Anthony, Bishop of Durham, 14,16,21,58,114
Bel, Jean le, chronicler, 54,69,70,71,78
Bemaken Priory, Isle of Man, 93,94,113
Benedict XII, Pope, 54
Berkeley Castle, 4,33
Berwick, 22,24,25,41-43,65,89,102,109
Bisham Priory/Abbey, 65,67,116,130,15; tombs in, 159,160

Black Death, 79,111,112
Bohemia, John, King of, 55,74
Bohun, William, 47,48
Bordeaux, 10,32,79,85,91,98,101,102,136,155,156
Boroughbridge, 32
Boughton House, 163
Bourges, 141,147,149,151
Brabant, Duke of, 50,54
Bren, Llewellyn, 25
Brétigny, Treaty of,
Bristol, 10,26,42,47,126,129
Brittany, 61,62,66,69,71,72,84
Bruce, David, see David II, King of Scots
Bruce, Robert, see Robert I, King of Scots
Bruges, Treaty of, 6,99,135
Bruton Priory, 26
Buccleugh, dukes of, 162-4
Buchan, John, Earl of, 142,147,148
Buchanan, Sir Alexander, 143,148
Burgundy, John 'The Fearless', Duke of, 135,140,141
Burgundy, Philip, Duke of, 141,142,146,150,151,154
Burne, Lt Col Alfred,147

Caerphilly Castle, 25,33
Calais, siege of, 3,74,75,76,77, treaty of, 90
Capetian family, 8,51
Cassington, Oxfordshire, 28,30,130
Castillon, battle of, 53,155,157
Castle Rushen, IoM, 4,22,24,29,58,94,95,113,114

175

Catherine of Valois, wife of Henry V, 138,141,144,147

Cecil family, 161,162

Charles, IV, King of France, 32

Charles V, King of France, 89,90,97,132,134

Charles VI, King of France, 109 110 120 138-142,144,157

Charles VII, King of France, 144,146,148,154,155

Charles, King of Navarre, 84,101

Chaucer, Alice, second wife of fourth Earl of Salisbury, 150,153

Chaucer, Geoffrey, 110,118,150

Chevauchées, 85,90,97,98,136,149

Clarence, George, Duke of, 158,159,160,161

Clarence, Thomas, Duke of, 131,136,141,142,143,148

Clement VI, Pope, 61,62,80,93,112

Clinton, William, Earl of Huntingdon, 47

Cravant, battle of, 146,147

Crécy, battle of 3,74,76,78,84,90,98,105,138

Creton, Jean, 126,127,130

Chandos, Sir John, and his herald, 85,86

Court of Chivalry, 107,110,128

'Chronicle of the Kings of Man and the Isles', 11,24,59

Damory, Roger, 28

Darnley, Sir John Stewart of, 146

Dauphin, 86,88-90,141,142

David II, King of Scots, 35,41,56,58,62,74,76,89,111

de Burgh, Richard, 13

de Dunois, Jean, 152

de la Mare, Sir Peter, 99

de Vere, Robert, Earl of Oxford, 107-9, 110,123

Denbigh, castle and lordship of, 38,39, 59,66,68,83,84,90,110,111,121,157

Derby, Earl of, see Henry IV

Despenser, Henry, Bishop of Norwich, 104,109

Despenser, Hugh the Elder, 28,30,32,33,48,83

Despenser, Hugh the Younger, 28,30,32,33,48

Donyatt, 15,72

Douch, Robert, 3

Douglas, Sir Archibald, 41,42

Drogo de Montagud, 15

Dunbar, 52,53

du Guesclin, Bertrand, 97,98

Dupplin Moor, battle of, 41

Edinburgh, 10

Edward I, King of England, 9,13,14,16,18, Oath of the Swans,19; death,20; 21,48,66,83

Edward II, King of England, not murdered?18; accession,20; 21-26,30, 32, abdicates, 33; 34,35,37,43,48,50, 51,65,70,108,114

Edward III, King of England, 3,5,6,born,20; coronation,33; 35-8,41-45,47,48,50-54, assumes arms of France, 55; 56-68, alleged rape of Countess of Salisbury,69-72; 73, Crécy,74; Calais,75,76; 77, the Garter, 78; 79, 80, 82-84, 88, 89, 90, 94, 96, 100; 105, 107,110,115, 135,136,157

Edward IV, King of England, 158,160

Edward VI, King of England, 160,162

Edward, Prince of Wales ('The Black Prince'),47,61,63,72,73,78, nickname,84; Poitiers,88,90; married Joan of Kent, 91; 97,death,100; 105,118,119

Eltham, John of, 40,68,71

Epiphany Rising, 129,130,132

176

Index of Main Items

Esplechin, Truce of, 56,71

France, map of and list of kings of, 73, population in 1300,9
Francis, Maud, wife of third Earl of Salisbury, 118,130,159
Florence of Worcester, chronicler, 10
'Flores Historiarum',18,29
Froissart, Jean, chronicler, 70,76,78,102,103,123,124

Gascony, 3,8,9,16,28,32,51,144,155
Glyndwr, Owain, 132,133,136
Gaunt, John of, see Lancaster, Duke of
Gaveston, Piers, 20-22, death of, 23; 28,33,48
Gloucester, Thomas, Duke of, 107,109,110,120,127,128,131
Gloucester, Humphrey, Duke of, 140,144,150,151
Good Parliament, 99,101
Grandison, Catherine, wife of first Earl of Salisbury, 35,48,68,69,159
Gransden, Dr Antonia,71
Gray, Sir Thomas, chronicler, 38
'Great Schism' in the Papacy, 108,109,113,140
Gregory XI, Pope, 99
Grosmont, Henry of: see Lancaster
Guyenne, 8,88

Halidon Hill, battle of, 42-44,53
Hawise, wife of Simon, Lord Montagu, 16
Hall, John, chronicler,150
Henry IV, King of England, previously Earl of Derby, Duke of Hereford and Duke of Lancaster, 103,110,119,121-127,129,130-134,136,137,143
Henry V, King of England, 4,6,133-6,137, Agincourt,138-140; 141-3, death,144; 159
Henry VI, King of England, 144,149,154,157-9
Henry VIII, King of England, 160,161
Hinchingbrooke House, 165
Hoby, Sir Philip, 160
Holland, Eleanor, first wife of fourth Earl of Salisbury, 131,153,156,159
Holland, Sir Thomas, Earl of Kent, 77,78,80,90,91
Holmes, Professor Geoffrey, 66
Hundred Years War, 6,50,begins,51; 53,135,155

Isabella of France, wife of Edward II, 20,21,32,33,35,37,38,51,52,72
Isle of Man, 3,4,6-14,16,17,22,23,29, granted to Montagus,41-4; 46,48,57-59, map of,60; 61,66,68,89,90,sale of,111; 112,116,132,157
Isle of Wight, 105,106,107

James I, King of Scots, 142
Joan of Arc, 4,154,155
Joan of Kent, 72,76,77,80,90,91,100
John II, King of France, 80,84,86,88,89,90,96,135,138
John XXII, Pope, 28,37
Justices of the Peace (JPs), 80,93,104,110

Kent, Edmund, Earl of, 37,72
Kent, Thomas Holland II, Earl of, 101,120
Kimbolton Castle, 164
Kings of Man, 10,11,58,59,82,112,114,115,121
Knighton, Henry, chronicler, 45
Knights Templar, 23,65,69,159

Lancaster, John of Gaunt, Duke of, 96-105,109-111,119,120,124,125

Lancaster, Thomas, Earl of, 23,28-30,death,32; 48,83,96

Le Mans, siege of, 149,150,153

Lewis IV, Holy Roman Emperor,50,54,61

Lewyn, John, architect, 121

Lionel, Duke of Clarence, 45,70,90,97,100,133

Lollards, 4,101,119,120

London (population in 1300),10

Lords Appellant, 110,118,119,127

Lydgate, John, poet, 153,155

MacAskil, Gilbert,21,24

MacDowall, Dungal, 22,24

Magnus, King of Man, 12,13

Malestroit, Truce of, 62

Man, see Isle of and Kings of

Manchester, Earls and Dukes of, 162-5

Mar, Earl of, 41

March, Earls of, 35,37,68,74,111,121,122,132

Mathew, Gervase, 119

Mohun, Elizabeth de, second wife of second Earl of Salisbury, 80,87,105,116,159

Montacute, 15,16

Montagu family, early history,15;arms,44

Montagu, Alice, daughter of fourth Earl of Salisbury, 156,159

Montagu of Beaulieu, Lords, 162,164

Montagu, Sir Edward, LCJ, 162,163

Montagu, Lord Edward, brother of first Earl of Salisbury, 66,71

Montagu, Simon, first Lord Montagu, 3,14,15,19, appointed admiral,21; imprisoned,22; 23, death,26

Montagu, Simon, Bishop of Ely, 57,66

Montagu, Lord John, brother of second Earl of Salisbury, 72,101,105,107, 108,118, his tomb,116,117

Montagu, John, Marquess of, 160

Montagu, William, first Earl of Salisbury, 3,4,born,30; knighted,33; married,35; embassy to Avignon,37; the Nottingham coup,37,38; lord of Denbigh,38; 40,41,granted IoM,42; 43,44,embassy to France,45; Scottish expedition,45; seal,46; admiral of the fleet,47; created Earl of Salisbury,47; blind in one eye,48; 49, at Dunbar,52; 53, his ships,54; marshal of England, 54; captured at Lille,55-6; and archbishop Stratford,57; crowned king of the IoM,58; 59,61-4,death,65; 66,assessment of,68; 69,71,72,115,159

Montagu, William, second Earl of Salisbury: see Salisbury, Earl of

Montagu, William, son of second Earl of Salisbury, 80,killed,105; 106,107,159

Montagu House, London, 163

Montford, Elizabeth, wife of second Lord Montagu, 17,30,31

Monthermer family, 68,115,116

Moray, Earls of, 29,41,43,52,58,59,62,76,82,111,114

Morley, Thomas, Lord,127,128,131

Mortain, Robert, Count of, 15

Mortimer, Dr Ian, 4,6,33,71

Mortimer, Roger, first Earl of March, 4,21,32,33,35,37,death,38; 68,72,83,96

Mortimer, Roger, second Earl of March, 83,89

Murimuth, Adam, chronicler, 63-5

Nájera, battle of, 91,97

Neville's Cross, battle of,74,76,82,111

Neville family, 120,132,159

Neville, Richard, fifth Earl of Salisbury, 156

Norman Conquest, 1066, 7,9,15

Northampton, William Bohun, Earl of,

178

Index of Main Items

47,48,50,53,57,62,72,80
Northampton, Treaty of, 35,41
Northumberland, Henry Percy, Earl of, 132,133,134
Nottingham Castle, 37,38

Order of the Garter, 78,79,90,136
Ordinances and Ordainers, 22,23,30,32,43
Orléans, 4,9,151,153
Ormrod, Professor W. Mark, 6,41,42,43,50,68,76

Packe, Michael, 71
Peasants' Revolt, 102,103,104,119
Perche, Count of, 141,142,157
Peel, IoM, 58,59,61,92,93,112,113
Perrers, Alice, 97,99
Perth, 12,13,45
Peter I, King of Castile, 80,91,98
Philip IV, King of France, 13,20,23,51
Philip V, King of France, 33,51
Philip VI, King of France, 35-7,40,44,45,50,51,54,56,61
Philippa of Hainault, wife of Edward III, 32,37,40,55,69,75
Phillips, Professor Seymour,18
Plantagenet family, 8
Poitiers, battle of, 3,86,88,90,98
Pole, Margaret, Countess of Salisbury, 160,161

Radcot Bridge, 110,123
Reginald I, King of Man, 11,12,94,95
Richard II, King of England, 31, born,100; crowned,101; Peasants' Revolt,102-104; 107-110,115,118-121, 122,123-128, death,132
Robert I, King of Scots, 18-20,22,24,25, 29,32,35,41,43,65

Robert III, King of Scots, 142
Round Table Feast, 64,65
Rushen Abbey, IoM, 11,112,115
Russell, William, Manx bishop, 93

Salisbury, earldom of, 4,48
Salisbury Cathedral, 84,116,117,145
Salisbury, John Montagu, third Earl of, 4,109,111,116,118,119, succeeds as earl,120; 121,123,125-132,138, 143,156,159
Salisbury, Richard Neville, fifth Earl of, 157,158,160
Salisbury, Richard Neville, sixth Earl of and sixteenth Earl of Warwick, ('Warwick the Kingmaker'), 157-160.
Salisbury, Thomas Montagu, fourth Earl of, 3,131,132,134,136, KG,136; 138-143,145,146,147-150,151,152, death,153; 154,155,156,159
Salisbury, William Montagu, first Earl of, see Montagu
Salisbury, William Montagu, second Earl of, 3,4,5,68,72,74, divorce from Joan of Kent,77; KG,78; 80,81,82,83,86,87, at Poitiers, 88; 89, assessment, 90; 91,CastleRushen, 93; 94,96-101, Captain of Calais,102; Peasants' Revolt,103; 104, kills his son,105; quarrel with heirs, 107; 108,111-15, 118,159
Sandwich, Earls of, 162,165,166
Saul, Professor Nigel, 118,123
Scrope, Sir William, Earl of Wiltshire, 111,115,120,121,123,125,125,133
Scotland, population in 1300, 9
Seton, Sir Alexander, 42
Shakespeare, William, 78,136,139
Sherborne Castle, 84,90
Shipton Montagu, 15
Sluys, naval battle of, 56
Stanley family, 112,114,133,134

179

Statute of Treasons, 83
Steward, Robert, 45,57
Stirling, 24,46,57,62
Stratford, John, archbishop, 56,57,76,82
Suffolk, Michael de la Pole, Earl of, 108,109,110
Suffolk, Robert Ufford, Earl of, 47,53-7,65,67
Suffolk, William de la Pole, Earl of, 149,150,153,154
Sumption, Jonathan, 6,53
Trastámara, Henry of, 91,98
Troyes, Treaty of, 142,144
'Tourelles', 152-4
Tournaments, 5,37,40,43,50,52,61,64,69,70,77,78,88,105,129
Tyler, Wat, 3,102,104
Tynwald, IoM, 61,112

Valois family, 51
Verneuil, battle of, 147-150

Walsingham, Thomas, chronicler, 119,120
Walworth, Sir William, 103,107
Wark Castle, 35,36,44,59,66,70,71,120,157
Warner, Dr Mark, 3,152,156
Warwick, Thomas Beauchamp, Earl of, 62,65,78,80,85,86,88,89,97,102,110,120,121
Wavrin, Jean de, chronicler, 147,148,153
Westmorland, Ralph Neville, Earl of, 132-4
Winchelsea, naval battle of, 80,90
Windsor Castle, 5,63,78,79,91,96,129
Wingfield, Sir John, 72,82,85
Wycliffe, John, 118,119

Wyvill, Robert, Bishop of Salisbury, 84

Yarlington, 30
York, 10,16,41
York, dukes of, 109,120,125,126,157,158